PRAISE FOR KEYS OF TRUTH

"*Keys of Truth* is a phenomenal depiction of the distinct gender differences that allow us to function in our God-given roles. Cristie Penn gets straight to the heart of the matter when it comes to relationships and makes understanding them very simple, yet allows for significant introspection and reflection. These gender-specific communication concepts are essential for every person to be successful in any type of relationship. *Keys of Truth* is such a delight to read and makes applying these deep concepts simple and understandable. I love that Cristie's heart is to see people walking freely in their true identity and as the best version of themselves. I will use this book with clients and in teaching students how to effectively counsel those they encounter, as well as in my own relationships. This is an excellent resource!"

Dr. Cassandra Reid, LPC-S, PhD
Founder, Cassie Reid Counseling
Director of Counseling Programming, The King's University

"What a fascinating read! Cristie has so eloquently outlined the core variances between male and female and how these differences affect every relationship we have. This book will revolutionize the way you interact with the opposite gender and will have a profound impact on your relationships."

Josh Morris
Associate Senior Pastor, Gateway Church
Dallas/Fort Worth, Texas

"My wife and I have been doing marriage counseling for the last 17 years, and the material in this book will definitely become a major part of our counseling going forward. Cristie has truly unlocked the keys of truth about men and women. Everyone interested in having a significant covenant relationship with his or her spouse will love this book."

Jim Pack
Founder and President of One Heart Ministry
Executive Pastor, City Life Church
Dallas/Fort Worth, Texas

"Cristie Penn's desire to see honor restored between men and women shines through. Her book attends to building successful relationships, and she has drawn a picture of how men and women can 'dance,' work, love, protect, collaborate and thrive together. In bringing her insight and understanding, she encourages the body of Christ in the practical keys of living in dignity, wisdom, and grace while partnering with one another."

Barbara Byers, PhD, Licensed Professional Counselor
Dallas/Fort Worth, Texas

"I've known Cristie Penn for 10 years and have seen the love she has for people and the desire God's given her to see men and women thrive in their relationships with one another. When I first heard her share about the keys of truth, I knew it was a fresh word that every man and woman across the globe needed to hear. As a pastor who's been ministering to women for more than 25 years, I am so thankful she's now put this information into a book for everyone to read."

Debbie Morris
Executive Pastor of Pink (Gateway Women), Gateway Church
Dallas/Fort Worth, Texas
Author of *The Blessed Woman* and Co-author of
The Blessed Marriage and *Living Rightside Up*

"What a breath of fresh air *Keys of Truth* is. In a time when the world around us seems lost in confusion in relation to gender roles, this book brings clarity and hope. *Keys of Truth* is easy to read, easy to understand, and easy to apply to our lives."

Steven Kaylor
Lead Pastor, Hope Church
Tokyo, Japan

"I first heard snippets of this message on the other side of the world while serving orphans with Cristie Penn in Zambia, Africa. My husband and I were struggling through some marriage issues, and Cristie spoke life to us. God has entrusted a powerful message to this mighty woman of God!"

Tammie Head
Bible Teacher and Author of *More* and *Duty or Delight?*

"Hopeful and empowered. That's how you'll feel when you spend time reading *Keys of Truth*. If you take to heart these truths and use them, even some of them, your marriage, friendships, and even work relationships will be transformed. I commend Cristie for being authentic enough to listen to the Lord and then translate what she's learned onto paper for all of our benefit!"

Lisa Rose
Founder of First Friday, and Founder and President of Gatehouse
Dallas/Fort Worth, Texas

"*Keys of Truth* is a Holy Spirit–inspired lesson that will enlighten you, challenge you, and change you. Read it knowing it's not too late to change. I'm thankful Cristie was obedient and allowed the Lord to use her to share truths that will help and heal. The life-changing keys in this book are straight out of God's Word."

Gary Randle
Co-founder/President of the Board, HOPE Farm
Fort Worth, Texas

"As a product of an unsuccessful marriage and two relationships, *Keys of Truth* has given me stable, Christian-based guidance on how to understand a man. It has also shown me the art of maneuvering around my insecurities with men. This book has mesmerized me. I've read it over and over and each time a new enlightenment is revealed. I cannot put it down and want to keep it near me for quick reference. It's a must read for every woman looking to have a successful and loving relationship, a manual for every marriage! Cristie was God inspired to reach women of all ages and backgrounds with words of encouragement for a better life. It has certainly moved and touched my soul, and I look forward to the day God gives me another opportunity to use what I've learned."

Eileen Salazar-Szep
Senior Executive Administrator to President & CEO,
Royal Caribbean International

"Today we face a crisis regarding the definition of marriage. Many have become confused and surrendered their dreams of one man and one woman for life to the lies and schemes of an enemy who wants to destroy biblical marriage. Now more than ever, we need strong mentors and clear voices that can communicate God's plan and purpose for healthy marriages. In *Keys of Truth: Unlocking God's Design for the Sexes*, Cristie Penn takes the discussion of gender to a new level. She serves as the master mentor, transparently sharing from her own life stories, offering keys to greater understanding of our identity in Christ and teaching us how to grow in our value and respect for the opposite sex. I highly recommend this book to anyone who desires to communicate more effectively, love more deeply, and build a lifelong love affair with his or her spouse."

Jan Greenwood
Pastor of Pink (Gateway Women), Gateway Church
Dallas/Fort Worth, Texas
Author of *Women at War*

"Passionate, determined, beautiful, humble, and full of compassion is how I would describe Cristie. I am not surprised about her desire to obey God's calling to write *Keys of Truth*. This book offers powerful insight to people who are married, single, and engaged and those who are seeking a relationship according to God's original design. This is an opportunity to rediscover and reposition your heart to unveil and reveal redemptive and practical truths about yourself and the majesty of God's love to restore and heal relationships."

Dorothy Newton
Speaker and Author of *Silent Cry*

"This book will certainly add Cristie Penn to the bibliographies in many books to come on the topic of biblical gender understanding. With creativity, she combines the wisdom of experience and the knowledge of valued research to equip men and women for more meaningful relationships. This is a book that you will not only read but will use for reference and recommendation frequently."

Devi Titus
Speaker and Author of *Home Experience*
Co-founder and Vice-President, Kingdom Global Ministries

"*Keys of Truth* offers new insights into the multifaceted challenge of communication between men and women. This message offers powerful lessons that will transform your relationships with the opposite sex and enhance your ability to communicate more effectively with both men and women."

Lynda Grove
Pastor of Pink (Gateway Women), Gateway Church
Dallas/Fort Worth, Texas

KEYS OF TRUTH

Unlocking God's Design for the Sexes

Cristie Penn

Keys of Truth: Unlocking God's Design for the Sexes

Published by Cristie Penn

Copyright © 2015 by Cristie Penn

Requests for information should be addressed to:

Cristie Penn, 401 N Carroll Ave, Suite 172, Southlake, TX 76092

Scripture marked (MSG) taken from The Message. Copyright © 1993, 1994, 1995, 1996, 2000, 2001, 2002. Used by permission of NavPress Publishing Group.

Scripture marked (NASB) taken from the NEW AMERICAN STANDARD BIBLE®, Copyright © 1960, 1962, 1963, 1968, 1971, 1972, 1973, 1975, 1977, 1995 by The Lockman Foundation. Used by permission.

Scripture marked (NIV) taken from THE HOLY BIBLE, NEW INTERNATIONAL VERSION®, NIV® Copyright © 1973, 1978, 1984, 2011 by Biblica, Inc.® Used by permission. All rights reserved worldwide.

Scripture marked (NKJV) taken from the New King James Version®. Copyright © 1982 by Thomas Nelson. Used by permission. All rights reserved.

Scripture quotations marked (NLT) are taken from the Holy Bible, New Living Translation, Copyright © 1996, 2004, 2007 by Tyndale House Foundation. Used by permission of Tyndale House Publishers, Inc., Carol Stream, Illinois 60188. All rights reserved.

Cover and Layout Design: Julie Kieschnick, Vine Printing

Cover Photography: Cory Hale

Because of the dynamic nature of the Internet, any web addresses or links contained in this book may have changed since publication and may no longer be valid.

Printed in the United States of America.

ISBN #978-194384614-6

For Don, my strong, yet gentle, husband and partner in life.

Thank you for partnering with God to provide for and protect
our family and me. My life and my relationship with you are
more than I ever dreamed or imagined. Thank you for not
giving up on us or me. Thank you for never ceasing to
war for us—no matter what came against you.

For our children—Jonathan and Holly.

You're even more amazing than I could have imagined.
Thank you for always providing innumerable opportunities
for me to learn, grow, and walk in authenticity.

And for all the men and women who want to
partner with God and experience the kind of
vibrant relationships He created them to enjoy.

*And this is my prayer: that your love may abound more
and more in knowledge and depth of insight, so that
you may be able to discern what is best and may be
pure and blameless for the day of Christ, filled with
the fruit of righteousness that comes through
Jesus Christ—to the glory and praise of God.*
Philippians 1:9–11 (NIV)

TABLE OF CONTENTS

FOREWORD BY ROBERT MORRIS

When Debbie and I first got married, we had a lot to learn about communication. I'd come home from work and she would immediately start bombarding me with questions. "Where were you?" "Who did you see?" "What did he say?" "What did you say?" "Why did it take so long?" It was just on and on. The whole time I was thinking, *She is the nosiest human being on the planet!*

If a guy had asked me, "How was your day?" I would have said, "Fine." And that would have been the end of the conversation. That would not work with her. I didn't realize it at the time, but the reason she was asking me so many questions was that God wired her with a *need* to communicate. And the reason she has to communicate is because it's how she relates with me. It wasn't that Debbie was nosy; it was that she wanted to *connect*.

It didn't take long before we decided we would set aside 30 minutes every night just to talk. We got into a practice of getting into bed, turning out the lights, and *talking*. This was "our time"— no kids, no distractions, just us. We'd share about our days, what we did, who we saw, everything. *We would connect to each other*, and after a while, I began to really like this time together.

Guys, once you've learned to connect with a woman (by the way, that's really why God put them in our lives), you can *really* connect with God. My relationship with God has gone so much deeper, and it's because I learned to connect with Debbie. That's why I'm so excited about *Keys of Truth*. This book will help men and women connect with one another and with God in a deeper way.

Debbie and I have been close friends with Don and Cristie Penn for many years. We've been with them on vacation, gone to dinner together, spent holidays together, and had a lot of fun over the years. We've also seen how Don's personality is very different from Cristie's, yet we know God created them to be *exactly* who they are. We've watched them interact lovingly and kindly and function as a team. Having been friends for so long, we've seen the fruit of their marriage and family.

Last year we were with Don and Cristie in their home, when Cristie began to share with us about how, through her relationship with Don, God revealed some principles—truths, really—that shed light on His design for the sexes. By the end of the night, we knew she had to put these teachings into a book and share them with as many people as possible. It was clear this was a message *everyone* needed to hear.

As a pastor, I care about how men and women view themselves and how they relate to one another in marriage, in the workplace, and in friendships. God created us to serve a purpose as individuals and in each other's lives. The principles in *Keys of Truth* are straight from God's Word and are crucial for teaching us how to connect and relate to one another the way He designed us. They will also help us live with and honor our spouses in a godly way.

Without understanding these truths, we fulfill Hosea 4:6, which says, "My people are destroyed for lack of knowledge." Many times we want to do the right things, but we don't know *how*. I believe God is going to speak to you through this book and reveal something you didn't know about yourself and the opposite sex.

Whether you're married, single, divorced, or widowed, *this book is for you*. I'm telling you, understanding these truths will change your life!

Robert Morris
Founding Senior Pastor, Gateway Church
Dallas/Fort Worth, Texas
Bestselling Author of *The Blessed Life*, *From Dream to Destiny*, *The God I Never Knew*, and *Truly Free*

NOTE FROM CRISTIE

W*elcome to the journey!* I'm so happy you've decided to come. I've been praying for you. With every stroke of the computer keys, I've had *you* on my mind. If you're single, married, divorced, a parent, or a grandparent—this book is for *you*. It's for anyone who does life with the opposite gender. I want so much for you to catch this message and grab hold of these keys of truth, because when you do, they can completely change your life and the lives of those you love.

Did you know that from the moment we were born, there has been an all-out war raging for our souls? God's enemy—Satan—wants to destroy us. He hates God, and because we are a reflection of Him, he hates us. Our value to the Almighty makes us shiny trophies to the enemy. Knowing that we are treasures to God should breathe confidence and courage into our souls. We are so important to Him that Satan tries to use *us* to hurt God's heart. There's only one problem: *Satan can't humiliate God.* But he can hurt Him by causing us to dishonor God or to *not* believe God is who He says He is and we are who God says we are to *Him*.

God doesn't *need* us, but He *desires* us. He created males and females to love and to love Him back—he wanted us to be His family. That's why, since the Garden of Eden, Satan has focused on destroying relationships between males and females. If he can tear us apart and pit us against one another, he knows that can destroy marriages, families, churches, communities, and civilizations. Yet, regardless of what the enemy tries to do or what current culture tries to make us believe, God had a plan for males and females from the very beginning, and He hasn't changed it.

Most of us have read books or attended conferences focusing on relationships between men and women. We often wonder if there could be anything new we haven't already heard. I'm not suggesting I have heard everything or have all the answers; however, I personally believe the truths you'll read in this book can break down confusion and frustration between the genders while bringing clarity and understanding. My husband, Don, and I are proof that when you activate these keys of truth by the power of the Holy Spirit, *they really do work!* They have proven to revolutionize lives and save failing relationships, build stronger partnerships, and repair friendships.

We all know that males and females are different, but few understand how to make our differences work *for* us. My hope is that this book will highlight the awesomeness of God's amazing plan and help us enjoy and appreciate one another.

While I may not have all the answers, I know the One who does. The Lord has graciously revealed lies I believed about myself, about others, and about Him. I write from a heart of gratitude to Jesus for His patience and presence along the way, even when I did not recognize Him. I believe God's Word is true and it holds the answers to all of life's questions, whether I understand it all or not. God wants to rescue, restore, equip, and transform all who are willing to pause, ponder, pray, and obey what He says.

Some of you who are reading this may be hurting, broken, and desperate. I want you to know that God doesn't waste pain. Often He uses our pain to get our attention and birth a teachable heart. He loves us desperately and chases us relentlessly. He longs for us to stop running from Him and instead turn and look at Him, face-to-face. He wants to see His children the way He created them—whole, satisfied, and content—but this only comes through a personal relationship with His son (John 14:6).

I can't tell you how excited I am to share what I have learned. May these keys of truth bring you peace as you realize that you are not *weird*, but you are *wired* a certain way—God's way!

I hope when you close the back cover of this book you will feel empowered and have a clearer understanding of yourself and the opposite gender. I pray the Lord will bless you with His heart and perspective as you journey all the way through.

Cristie Penn

*Before you continue reading this book, I would love for you to visit my website at **keysoftruth.org** and watch the special video message I prepared just for you!*

What you say goes, God, and stays, as permanent as the heavens. Your truth never goes out of fashion; it's as up-to-date as the earth when the sun comes up. Your Word and truth are dependable as ever; that's what you ordered—you set the earth going. If your revelation hadn't delighted me so, I would have given up when the hard times came. But I'll never forget the advice you gave me; you saved my life with those wise words. Save me! I'm all yours. I look high and low for your words of wisdom. The wicked lie in ambush to destroy me, but I'm only concerned with your plans for me. I see the limits to everything human, but the horizons can't contain your commands!
Psalm 119:89–96 (MSG)

This book is written to be more like a manual or guidebook, offering instructions that will bring new and different results to every relationship in your life. The layout is designed for you to read quickly so you can implement a key or two at a time. It's also designed for those who may not have as much time to read. If this is you, pick a section or chapter that applies to you and start there!

NOTE FROM DON

When Cristie and I first got married, we were just two kids in love. We didn't put much thought into how our marriage was going to work and, as scary as it may sound, it was a mystery waiting to unfold. The first few years of our marriage were great. Then when our two children were added to the dynamic, all of a sudden, life got *real*. The next several years we switched from being just husband and wife to being parents, and our relationship took a backseat as all of our attention focused on the children.

After the kids grew up and became more independent, Cristie began to feel alone and vulnerable. We'd spent years of neglecting our marriage, and now things were beginning to spiral out of control. Cristie tried everything she could to get my attention, but to me it felt like she was trying to control me. The more she tried to reach me, the more resentful and defensive I became. I felt emasculated and pulled away from her even more. Our marriage was dangling from a string, yet we knew divorce wasn't an option for us. We'd made a commitment to one another, and we'd both grown up with parents who had imperfect marriages but stayed together. For better or for worse, we knew that's what we had to do. Yet the downward spiral continued. We pulled further away from each other as I focused more on work, and Cristie stayed busy being a mom and leading Bible studies. We were stuck in a horrible cycle.

Then, it all began to change.

God started revealing to Cristie things she needed to do or say to connect with me. These truths the Lord showed her were so powerful yet so simple to understand and apply. She followed the Lord's leading and began changing the way she was communicating with me and relating to me. The change in our marriage was dramatic: Trust was restored, communication lines that had been closed for years (or actually never existed) were opened, and our hearts started softening toward each other. God revealed to us the vast chasm our marriage had become *and* what He intended our marriage to be, and the difference was *remarkable*.

As Cristie began to share with me what the Lord had been revealing to her, I was riveted. Gradually, I began to grasp the keys of truth the Lord was showing her, and I began to see *her* differently. I was seeing her the way God made her. And it was because she was treating me in a way that allowed me to understand her better. I no longer felt threatened or challenged, I felt affirmed and honored. Her words and actions were life to me.

I wish I had understood that God designed Cristie to need my covering and every time I pulled away, she felt she was losing her security and tried harder to get my attention. She wasn't trying to *control* me; she was trying to *connect* with me. I never realized she only wanted my covering, and, by God's design, I was inherently wired to provide that for her. Understanding how God wired us and made us to work together was revolutionary to me and to our relationship! Once I had personally experienced these keys and began to understand Cristie and myself in new ways, I knew others needed to know and understand these keys of truth.

I hope everyone reads this book but especially young couples before they're married. If they do, they'll have a better understanding of each other from day one, and I know from experience how valuable that is. Men need to feel like men and women need to feel like women, both covering and connecting with each other as God planned. This is the fulfillment God intended for marriage.

Just as a mustard seed is extremely small but very powerful, these keys of truth are very simple and show us what God intended for our relationships to look like. If applied, they can change your life, your marriage, your working relationships, and your friendships. As you read this book, I believe you'll begin to understand the way the opposite sex responds to and acts toward certain things isn't by choice—it's God's design.

Don Penn

And do not be conformed to this world, but be transformed by the renewing of your mind, that you may prove what is that good and acceptable and perfect will of God.
Romans 12:2 (NKJV)

Chapter 1

THE REVELATION

The fact that Don and I are still married after 36 years is truly a miracle. Like most couples, we walked out of the chapel and into our future high on love yet completely unaware of the personal wounds we both brought along for the journey. Full of excitement, we ignorantly launched into uncharted territory, never realizing there were storm clouds billowing in the distance.

We had not considered God or His plan for our marriage; we just wanted to build a good and honest life. Yet both of us carried

Not only were there actual storm clouds on our wedding day, there was also three inches of ice on the ground, which would prove to be prophetic.

unspoken and unrealistic expectations and misconceptions about marriage. We had huge voids in our hearts and because we didn't have personal relationships with Christ, we had no concept of *absolute truth*, which would later almost destroy us, not just as a couple but individually.

We were both raised by hardworking, honest parents and grew up in moral homes. My family was actively involved in church every week but Don's was not. Yet even though we went to church, our denomination didn't teach that Satan is real or that every story in the Bible is true, so in some ways we were ignorant and arrogant. Neither of us were aware there was an enemy whose goal is to kill or destroy us, and we certainly weren't equipped to fight against him.

For the first six years of marriage, we buried ourselves in our careers—I opened an interior design business while Don finished college and went to work for an engineering firm. By our seventh year of marriage, we decided to start our family. It wasn't long after that I closed my business and focused on being a wife to Don and a mom to our kids, Jonathan and Holly.

Being a stay-at-home mom was one of the hardest things I have ever done and by far the most valuable. I was trying to find my new identity, and the learning curve was extreme. I was selfish, lost, confused, and miserable. I was accustomed to dressing up every day and running my business. I was accustomed to calling the shots and thinking I was in control. This was the start of a season where the Lord began to break my strong sense of self-sufficiency. With me staying at home, Don had the pressure of trying to make up my half of our income. Then, just a few years later, Don opened his own engineering firm, which required long hours. The decision for me to stay home was a high price for us, but it was the right decision for our family at the time.

THE BEGINNING

When Jonathan was two years old, I went to an Easter pageant with his babysitter, Sally. As I watched an actor depict Jesus and the crucifixion, I realized I had *no idea* who Jesus was. Watching Him being tortured to death was horrifying! It was the first time I ever considered *what* He did *for me*. I went home and cried for hours. I wasn't sure what happened to me that night, but I knew I would never be the same.

Even though I'd gone to church my whole life, I did not own a Bible *or* understand the Word of God. For the next three years, I continued going to the church I was raised in, because I didn't think my family, including my husband, would understand if I went somewhere else. I didn't have a *spiritual root system* or a deep relationship with Jesus, so when a storm blew in, I was tossed around like a volleyball. During this time, my dad, mom, and sister (my only sibling) were each diagnosed with cancer, all within three years of each other. I felt like my life was unraveling.

Out of desperation, I accepted a friend's invitation to attend Bible Study Fellowship (BSF), a weekly Bible study. BSF and my teacher, Donna, taught me how to pray aloud and how to open up God's Word and *really* study it. I began to get to know Jesus personally, and I fell head over heels in love with Him. My dad, mom, and sister successfully completed cancer treatments, then my mom died suddenly from congestive heart failure. Her funeral would be the last day of my first year of BSF. I was 36 years old.

● ● ●

My mom passed away during a time my parents were not speaking to me because of my faith. People asked me back then if that devastated me, and, surprisingly to them, my answer was "no." My mom's anger toward me was because of my faith, and I believed she was no longer disappointed in me because she now knew Jesus was who I said He was.

As Jesus continued to change my heart and I grew closer to Him, my language and behavior changed. However, after 14 years of marriage, I never could have imagined what happened next. Because of my faith, Don also began to change—but not in the way I expected. He became distant and withdrawn. We started fighting about petty, insignificant things, and he grew increasingly frustrated with me to the point, at times, he became verbally abusive. Most of the time, he disconnected from me and neglected me, and our marriage, completely.

We lived around the corner from my parents and that didn't make things any better. Even before my mom passed away, my parents were very upset that I attended a nondenominational Bible study. They told me I had gone off the deep end and had become a "Jesus freak." My parents repeatedly told Don I was unstable and was "doing damage" to our kids; they even accused me of being in a cult. My dad told Don he should take the kids and divorce me just to get my attention and make me "snap out of it." Don trusted and respected my dad and thought he might be right. This only caused him to become more confused and frustrated with me. Because Don had not yielded his life to Christ at the time, the enemy used my family to gain a foothold and try to destroy our marriage. (And he *almost* succeeded!) I felt violated, betrayed, ambushed, and completely alone, which only pushed me to press deeper into Jesus. All I could do was pray and trust God with my future.

Dear friends, do not be surprised at the fiery ordeal that has come on you to test you, as though something strange were happening to you. But rejoice inasmuch as you participate in the sufferings of Christ, so that you may be overjoyed when his glory is revealed.
1 Peter 4:12–13 (NIV)

For years, the spiritual battle in our home was profuse and exhausting. There were times I could hardly breathe; I was filled with so much fear and pain. Even though we'd had relational struggles in our marriage before I was saved, it was much worse afterward. We had never fought like *this*. Both of us felt like our hearts were being ripped to shreds. I didn't understand what was happening but neither did Don. He felt like the woman he had married was gone and that scared him. A cavernous rift stretched between us and was growing deeper and wider by the day.

Part of the problem was I had developed some *false beliefs* that caused me to shut down. I falsely believed Christian women were to figuratively wash the feet of their husbands, faithfully serve them, and pray for their salvation, *in silence*. I also falsely believed if I did that, Don would come to Christ. I assumed every Christian woman I knew had a perfect husband. I had not been around many Christian men and had a false idea of what they were like. I thought it was my responsibility to be an example to my entire family, which made me perform, desperately trying to be "the perfect Christian woman." God later showed me this was impossible and wrong.

What God wanted was for me to be authentically focused on Him and believe that those who wanted Jesus would automatically follow, because He would draw them to Himself. I was to model Jesus to my family, but the focus was not on me or my perfection, the focus was to be on *Him*. I had assumed if I wanted those I loved to come to the Lord, it was up to me to be Jesus to them. This may have sounded good on the surface, but over time, when I did not see any change, I became angry and bitter at Don, God, and myself. I had fallen into a trap. I knew God *could* save Don and fix our marriage, because he had saved me. I wanted so much to have a healthy, God-focused marriage and home for our precious children and believed God wanted this too, so why didn't he answer my prayers? Was I not faithful enough? Trusting enough? Praying enough? Being "good" enough? It sounds ridiculous now, but I really did wonder.

Over time, Don's emotional neglect and absence brought

fear, which caused me to self-protect and isolate myself from him. I was crawling deeper and deeper into an emotional hole. Later I would realize I had not only *lost my voice* but also my *identity*. I have learned since that in the midst of all the years of chaos, Don's behavior and response was the only way he knew how to "shake me awake." He wanted to get back the fun girl he married. I had no idea he felt like he'd lost me or that he even cared. As I pulled away emotionally and grew into a quiet, passive female, our partnership broke and our relationship suffered. I stopped being the fun, exciting girl he fell in love with. This "new me" did not make my husband want to become a follower of Christ. To him, I'd become a robot, a shadow of the woman he once knew.

I didn't mean for it to happen. I thought I was doing the right thing, and it was God's will for me to force myself into being holy. Growing up, I had always held the role of the "good girl," so I tried doing everything I could to keep up this appearance, but it was exhausting. I thought if I spent time in God's Word, Don would see the change in me and would want to become a Christian. I did not understand it would take a supernatural work of the Holy Spirit and had nothing to do with me. I also didn't realize what I was doing was a form of manipulation of Don *and* God. God clearly had a lot of work to do in me.

He was also working on Don, but it would happen in His way and in His time. Remember my friend who invited me to BSF? Well, her husband invited Don to the men's group, and, just like me, Don got to know Jesus personally and fell in love with Him. It became evident God had His hand on Don all along.

In all this you greatly rejoice, though now for a little while you may have had to suffer grief in all kinds of trials. These have come so that the proven genuineness of your faith—of greater worth than gold, which perishes

> *even though refined by fire—may result in praise,*
> *glory and honor when Jesus Christ is revealed.*
> 1 Peter 1:6–7 (NIV)

THE ROAD TO FREEDOM

By now, Don was running a thriving engineering company, and together we stayed busy raising our kids. We loved this season, but honestly, we knew we had not yet unpacked our personal baggage or found freedom from years of family drama and battling against each other. What made our situation worse was, apart from the co-dependent entanglement of my family, Don and I didn't know who we were.

I had always been close to my dad and was very much a "daddy's girl." My mom's death, along with my dad's increasing health issues, brought a temporary reconciliation to our relationship. I loved being his caregiver, even though it was hard watching him suffer. But after a while, it became difficult to care for my family while taking care of him at the same time. Trying to be two places at once was taking a toll on me and our marriage. To help make things easier, we built a small house for him on our property so we could be near him *and* he could have his independence. However, it didn't take long—just a couple of years—for it to become clear that he still did not agree with our lifestyle or our priorities in Christ. He continually criticized Don and me in front of our children, which brought division, pain, and confusion. He threatened our marriage by demanding to have control of me—*just like he always had.*

We sought godly counsel and began to set boundaries for the first time in our lives, but he did not honor or respect the boundaries *or* my husband and his position. My dad rebelled against God and threatened to retaliate. I obeyed the Lord and stood firm with Don. I had to trust that God "had this" and hoped He would fix things and do a work in my dad's heart. Sadly, it did not end the way I had prayed, hoped for, and believed—it was quite the opposite. It was horrible. My dad chose to retaliate in a *very* ugly way and would eventually choose to disown us when the kids were adolescents.

I thought this experience with my dad would kill me, but you know what? It didn't. Instead, it grew me, changed me, and built great courage in me. Persecution from the world doesn't hurt nearly as bad as family persecution does. God freed our family from that legacy and gave us a new one. We all learned by close proximity how destructive rebellion against God could be, and it changed us. Rebellion can be *very expensive!* We reap what we sow, and that experience *dramatically* changed the way our little family sows!

When my father and my mother forsake me, then the Lord will take care of me. Teach me Your way, O Lord, and lead me in a smooth path, because of my enemies. Do not deliver me to the will of my adversaries; for false witnesses have risen against me, and such as breathe out violence. I would have lost heart, unless I had believed that I would see the goodness of the Lord in the land of the living. Wait on the Lord; be of good courage, and He shall strengthen your heart; wait, I say, on the Lord!
Psalm 27:10–14 (NKJV)

That was a very lonely time for us—as individuals, as a couple, and as a family. Try as they may, none of our friends could relate to *that* kind of pain. Some Christians couldn't understand how we could allow my dad to leave and disown us. (Not that we had a choice.) Thankfully, we received godly counsel from our church leadership, which gave us courage to do it God's way. During the worst part of the battle, I spent days with my face to the floor begging God to help me know what He wanted us to do. The Lord just kept whispering to my heart, "If you want your children to respect you and to know Me, you have to do exactly as I say. Even if it feels like it will kill you and you don't understand." So I chose to do exactly what He said, obey the Word of God, and rely on the provision and protection of my husband. Because of our obedience, God brought a freedom to our marriage and our family we had never experienced before, demonstrating once again that He can use *anyone* and *anything* He chooses to change our hearts and lives. Everything God spoke to me proved to be true even though He didn't do it the way I expected, but He did keep every promise He made to me during that time. We lost a lot but gained so much more.

A HEART SHIFT

As the dust settled, we changed churches and joined Gateway Church in Southlake, Texas, where we went through freedom ministry. (It *finally* felt like I wasn't crazy after all!) After a few years passed and the kids were both away at college, Don and I were asked to begin a Bible study for men and women. I had been hosting and leading Bible studies for women in our home for many years but had not included men before now. We talked about it and agreed it was the right time.

● ● ●

Freedom Ministry is a process fulfilling Jesus' mission as described in Luke 4:18-19. It encompasses various ministries that promote the activities described in this passage: preaching Good News to the poor, opening blind eyes, releasing captives and prisoners, and proclaiming the favorable year of the Lord. Freedom is the ability to respond fully to God out of who He created and redeemed you to be. Core lies, soul wounds, demonic oppression, and life patterns are all obstacles that can stand in the way of the life of freedom Jesus has made available to every believer. Freedom ministry is kingdom-focused and designed to help you learn to hear and respond to God's voice. As you identify and remove those things that are currently hindering your growth, you have the opportunity to enter the life you were made for, discover your identity in Christ, and learn how to be an influence in the lives of others.[1]

During this season, the Lord began to cause a shift deep within my heart. One night we were having Bible study upstairs at our house. There were about 40 people in the room when I sensed the Lord say, "Cristie, open your eyes." (God was about to rock my world!) Supernaturally, He began to raise the veil that had separated me from His truth about men and women. As I looked around the room, the women's faces faded, and I began to see the men in a brand new way. I saw men who wanted to be godly men. Men who wanted to follow God, lead their wives and families, and get it right *for the Lord*. I saw men who wanted to be helpful, strong, courageous, protective, and productive providers. I saw men who wanted to serve. As I continued to watch them worship, the Lord spoke to my heart again, this time saying, "And, by the way, they are a lot more afraid of failure than any woman in this room knows."

God always reveals to heal, and He began to show me He had more lies to uncover. Was it possible, because of my dad, I had become afraid of men and didn't trust them? Had I picked up another false belief in which strong, godly women don't need anyone or anything except Jesus? Had I started believing that women were to be strong and independent, know how to wield a sword, and fight for themselves? Was it possible Christian women had unknowingly been influenced by the world and had begun fighting *against* men instead of *partnering* with them? Had I become one of these women? I began to pray and ask God if it was possible the enemy had convinced men and women we don't need each another, and we were to be adversarial toward one another, as though we were on opposite teams. Did Satan, the author of confusion, want our focus to be on protecting ourselves so we didn't notice what he was doing?

• • •

A Christian woman needs Jesus *and* needs to be strong, but a woman wielding a sword of self-protection can intimidate and emasculate a man and cause him to lay down his sword, especially when she is glaring at *him*. Women have great power, but God never intended them to wield it at the expense of men. The same is true for men. They are endowed with great power, but it was never to be used at the expense of women.

Here's the truth God wanted me to see: Women are designed by God to need men and men are designed by God to need women. (Pink and blue *really* do make purple—the color of royalty!) **When we learn about our divinely designed differences and take our positions as males and females, we can walk confidently in our strengths. We are a reflection of God when we take our places and stand together as partners.**

This revelation came when I was training men and women to lead and facilitate our growing Bible study as couples. I began to *see men* the way God created them, and *they* began to step up and serve with strong, tender confidence. The men led very differently than women. It was a beautiful thing to watch. But, once again, the Lord was only getting started with the surgery he was doing in my heart. I saw men as strong and trustworthy, but truthfully, I didn't feel this way about Don, because I knew he could hurt me. I knew it would take much more courage and vulnerability on my part. I justified it and made excuses to God saying, "Don and I are better than ever, right? We are leading and studying the Bible together. Don't *You* think things are great?" But deep in my heart, I knew Don and I were not as close emotionally as I would like. Evidently, the Lord agreed!

By now, our nest was empty. It was just us. Jonathan had graduated from college in California and was working for a television network in Hollywood. Holly was attending Baylor University and loving life. While Don and I were still a work in progress, God had seemed to answer almost every prayer we'd prayed for the kids up to this point.

Then one weekend Holly brought a new *friend* home. His name was Jon. I wondered if he might be "the boy" I had been praying for since she was three. We loved watching the way this young man treated our daughter. He pursued her with everything he had. She was obviously stepping into a new position with him, and it was a time of discovery for us all as we watched them fall in love right before our eyes.

However, during their courtship I began to sense a sadness come and settle deep in my heart. At the same time, I also began to experience what I call "Holy Spirit flybys." You know, the feeling you get when the Lord is up to something but you aren't exactly sure what it is? A *knowing* He is focused on something in your heart or soul, but hasn't pressed on it enough to make you *have to* pay attention. I would flippantly ask the Lord, "What is this? What do You want?" But He wouldn't tell me, so I ignored it. After a few months, I began to take the feelings and questions into my quiet time (my personal, daily time with God). I would ask, but He was silent. This cycle went on for more than a year.

Then one Sunday afternoon, Jon drove into town without Holly. He had called ahead to see if Don and I were available to talk. Sure enough, He asked us if we would give him our blessing to ask Holly to be his wife. All three of us cried tears of joy, and Don and I said, "Yes!" The proposal was a surprise to Holly, but a family affair for both sides. Planning the wedding with Holly was a joy! The wedding weekend came, and we felt God's delight and pleasure over the entire event. It was like a dream and more than we could have asked for. God's presence was evident, and we felt His delight over Holly and Jon.

Then, once the ballroom was empty, the candles were blown out, the flowers were gone, and the bride and groom were on their honeymoon, God came into my quiet time and *finally* said, "Cristie, this sadness you have been feeling all this time is *grief*. This has nothing to do with Holly and her prince charming but more to do with the way you view *yours*." God reminded me of the way Jon looked at Holly and the way Holly responded to Jon. He was her hero, and he knew it. It had been decades since Don and I had looked at each other in this way. Where had my prince gone? More importantly, what had I done that led him to step away from his position? It broke my heart to think about how much things had changed between us.

If I was honest, I saw Don as a knight and a warrior, only instead of warring *for* me and *defending* me, he was across the arena on his horse with his shield and sword drawn, *opposing* me. In fact, most of the time we were opposing one another, trying to see who would knock the other off their horse first and win. So what had changed us?

I scooted closer to the Lord in my spirit and began to search His word, be still, and listen carefully. I searched for the truth and asked Him for the courage to see what He wanted to show me. It was as though the Father lovingly pulled me up into His lap, held me close, and began to show me His heart. What I saw was unexpected and shocking. While the revelation I received brought pain and a heavy burden, it also came with many opportunities for healing and restoration.

God asked me, "Do you believe Don is a kind man with good intentions? Hadn't he once swept you off of your feet? Do you believe he still wants the best for you and your family? Do you believe he loves you?" Then He asked me the biggest question of all, "Is Don still the most valuable gift I have ever given to you?" Of course, I said "Yes" to every question He asked.

I knew I had a choice to make. Would I stop running and allow the Lord to unlock a door in my heart that had been locked for years? I suddenly understood I could not change Don—and God only knows how hard I had tried. I began to recognize that with God's help, I *could* change the way I saw him if I would yield myself to the Holy Spirit and choose to *really* trust Him.

God didn't stop there. He continued by asking me some more difficult questions:

• Will you stop protecting yourself?

• Will you choose to be vulnerable with Don even if this causes you pain? Will you do this for Me?

• Will you choose to trust Me and do the "next right thing" as I direct you?

Fear ripped through me. *What if Don hurt me again, shut down, or verbally and emotionally attacked me? I might not be able to take it again. What if I put it all on the line and nothing changed?* The kids were on their own, which took away all my distractions. I had nowhere to hide. It was just the two of us ... I *was so afraid.*

Suddenly, I began to see the faces of the countless women I had ministered to (and with) for the past 20-plus years. As their faces flipped through my mind, I noticed something familiar about the way they each looked. God showed me that, like me, many of them had been "faking it." They made it *look* like everything was great on the outside. Inside, they were lonely, hurt, angry, and in some cases, bitter. They too had been hoping when their nest was empty there would be connection with their husbands, something they wanted more than anything. Sadly, the opposite was often true because of all the damage that had been done over so many years.

That day the Lord began revealing some things that are *still* astounding to me. He began showing me the "next right thing" to do, and I did them as He directed. They weren't hard, but they would take more than a little courage on my part. I began to obey the Holy Spirit, one thing at a time. These things began to change the way I viewed Don. This led to changing the way I spoke to him and treated him. Gradually, this brought trust in his heart toward me. Instead of defending himself *to* me, he began to partner *with* me. After about six months of listening to the Lord and unselfishly following His direction, Don let me know he liked what I was doing. Obeying God by applying His truths changed our lives and our marriage from the inside out, and it's better than we ever expected.

THE KEYS OF TRUTH

The whole time I had been praying for God to change Don, but God was waiting on me. He knew I had to leave my position of self-protection and self-provision, lay down my sword of defense, and allow Don to be my warrior and my king. I had to choose to believe we *both* wanted it to work. Once I began to obey the Lord and position myself to more deeply trust in and depend on Him, He was able to deal with Don's heart and bring about change in our marriage.

———————— ● ● ● ————————

For years, I wanted Don to know the Jesus who had found and rescued me. One morning during my quiet time, God began to show me a picture of something deep within my heart.

I was pulling a little red wagon up a well-traveled, muddy hill. I was sweating as I strained to pull with all of my might to bring the wagon up the hill. I knew God was at the top of the mountain, and I had been making regular visits to see Him and talk to Him. When I took a closer look, I could see the wagon I was desperately trying to pull was sinking in the mud because the load was too heavy. To my surprise, the heavy load was Don as a little boy! He was sitting in the back of the wagon I was pulling. He had on royal blue shorts and cowboy boots. He was facing the back looking down the mountain and dragging his boots in the mud. The more his boots became caked with mud, the harder it was for me to pull. He seemed to be oblivious to my struggle; instead, he was focused on how cool the caking mud was on his boots. Then, I heard what sounded like the Lord speak from the top of the mountain, "Cristie, drop the handle of the wagon. Let it go." I was so afraid to let it go! If I dropped the handle, what would happen to Don? We hadn't reached the top of the mountain yet. He might never know God the way I wanted him to! Then, the Lord spoke, "If you don't drop the handle you're not trusting me, *and* you are in My way! Sometimes when Don is cruel to you, it's because he's angry with Me. You are standing between us, and I can't get to him. With you in the way, he can't see Me."

That day, I chose to drop the handle of the wagon and let God speak to Don just as He had spoken to me. I learned we are sometimes mistreated and get hit in crossfire, because we are standing in a place that isn't ours. I'm not saying I'm never tempted to pick up the handle again, but I've learned to trust God with what He's doing in our lives. It's not my responsibility; it's between God and Don.

The things I began doing are what we now call *keys of truth.* These simple revelations about males and females impacted our marriage, our friends, and our adult children so much that Don encouraged—yes, even kindly pushed—me to write them down to share with others. I believe the Lord didn't give me these keys just for our marriage but for the Bride of Christ (the Church) globally. If God can use these keys of truth for us—an emotionally closed, disengaged, highly intelligent mechanical engineer who married a hypersensitive, broken, abandoned interior designer with family baggage—He can use them for anyone.

These keys of truth come from a place of pain, brokenness, and gratitude. Don and I did so much wrong even in trying to get it right. I learned I don't have to be or do anything for Jesus to love me. If my heart's desire is to know Him better and love Him more, He will use my life as a catalyst to draw people to Himself. I learned my walk with the Lord is like a high wire over the Grand Canyon. I am walking across and Jesus is in front of me, walking backward. He is calmly saying, "Look at My face, don't look away." I realized if I keep my eyes locked on His face, I won't be looking from side to side or behind me to see if my family or friends are coming. I don't have to perform the role of the good girl who leads everyone to Jesus. My part is to focus on Jesus, be the best, most authentic version of myself I can be, and His love and presence will draw people to Him. He wants us to be who He created us to be, continue to walk out our salvation, and trust Him with the details.

The change in our marriage didn't happen overnight. It took time to unpack everything we thought we knew, get freedom, go to professional Christian counseling, be teachable, believe the best about one another, and completely open our hearts to change. I am sharing from a position of imperfection, but if God can change our hearts and reposition *us*, I believe He can do the same for you. **He can transform any heart that is teachable and yielded to Him.** God is good and wants us to be so much more than we could ever imagine. Rest in Him and know He wants to partner with you. He wants success for you, because He loves you more than you can comprehend.

I hope as you read this book, you'll begin to understand and accept men and women in their God-ordained positions. I pray these keys of truth will help you live a life that is more vibrant and rewarding than you ever thought possible. Doing life God's way gives us confidence, power, and a strong, considerate voice while confirming our true identity.

I am so much stronger than I ever knew I could be. I now know I am a valued, precious, powerful child of the King. I know and believe He is who He says He is and I am who He says I am to Him. It really doesn't matter what others say about me or how good I am or am not; obedience to Him is what He is after. I have found my voice, and He has given me something to say. When we listen to the heart of our Heavenly Father, He will give us something to say that others need to hear. Knowing Him and knowing *our true selves* will give us the courage to say it. Let's be brave!

WARNING! Satan is the enemy of God and the enemy of your soul (mind, will, and emotions), and he doesn't want you to read this book because he doesn't want you free. He will do everything he can to keep you from finishing. I want to encourage you to press on and press in to the very end.

PAUSE, PONDER, PRAY, AND OBEY

At the end of each chapter, I've put together questions and activations to help you dig deeper into the Word and hear what the Lord is speaking to you. These questions and activations can be used for personal study as well as small group Bible studies.

- **PAUSE:** Stop, wait, and ask the Lord to speak to you about what you are reading.

- **PONDER:** Take time to think about what you believe and why you believe it. Look in God's Word and see if it aligns with what you have believed.

- **PRAY:** Take time to pray and ask the Lord to confirm or deny what you believe. Ask Him if you need to make some changes in the way you think. Then wait. You may not physically wait in that exact location or position, but in your spirit continue to pray and wait on the Lord to speak to you. It may be through music, a sermon, scripture, a person, or a situation. Keep praying, waiting, and expecting Him to share His heart with you.

- **OBEY:** When you have heard from the Lord and are sure it's God speaking (sometimes we have to wait on confirmation), make some personal notes, and then courageously obey what you sense He's asking you to do, even if it's hard or you're afraid and don't fully understand *why* or *how* it will turn out.

● ● ●

Sometimes we find a verse, claim it as a promise, and expect a *specific* result, but it doesn't always end the way we expected or wanted it to. It's important to remember the Lord is the one who *begins* and *finishes* our stories. He has a plan, and our part is to *choose* to trust Him. It's not over until He says it's over.

Before you continue, take a moment, find a quiet place, and pray the following prayer (aloud if you are comfortable):

Lord,

As I hold this book in my hands, give me a teachable heart and the ability to absorb what You want to say to me. I may have beliefs that are shaping the way I think that are not aligned with You. If so, expose them! In some ways, this book may seem countercultural and the enemy, Satan, may try to bring confusion to keep me from pressing through to the end. Show me quickly when he is at work against what You want to do.

Show me any critical or cynical areas in me and replace them with Your wisdom. Help me surrender my soul (mind, will, and emotions) to what You want to do. If there are sections in this book that seem contrary to what I believe, pull me close and show me what *You* think about them. Lord, our culture seems confused, in pain, and full of fear. Sadly, the lies of the enemy have seeped into the Bride of Christ, and she is suffering. If You want to use this book to bring the genders back to Your original design, give me the desire and courage to read it and apply it to *my* life. Show me the lies about my gender *and* the opposite gender that may have been passed down for generations in my family. Infuse me with a clear understanding that "we are all products of our environment," but Jesus Christ *reveals to heal* and *set us free*.

Give me passion and courage as I walk through this journey with my heart and eyes wide open. Bring truth and transparency as You free me to become who You created me to be.

In the mighty name of Jesus, I pray,

Amen

What is the Holy Spirit saying to you? Take some time to find three scripture verses that encourage you or confirm what you are hearing.

_____

_____

_____

_____

_____

_____

_____

_____

_____

_____

_____

_____

_____

_____

_____

_____

_____

_____

_____

_____

_____

_____

_____

_____

_____

_____

_____

_____

_____

_____

_____

_____

_____

_____

_____

_____

_____

_____

_____

*For our present troubles are small and won't last very long.
Yet they produce for us a glory that vastly outweighs them
and will last forever! So we don't look at the troubles we
can see now; rather, we fix our gaze on things that cannot
be seen. For the things we see now will soon be gone,
but the things we cannot see will last forever.*
2 Corinthians 10:3–6 (MSG)

Chapter 2

THE BURDEN

Recently, Don and I had the privilege of building a new home. Having owned an interior design firm and having built homes in the past, I was familiar with being on a construction site. So when I made daily trips to the job site to meet with subcontractors or to check on the progress, it didn't feel strange to me. But the experience was definitely different this time.

Early into the project, I became fascinated by what I was seeing and was quite surprised by how it was affecting me. I would walk the property every day, meeting with the project manager or builder. There was a constant flurry of activity. Whether the men were in the lot moving dirt, hoisting lumber to frame the house or set heavy beams, pulling electrical wires in the hot attic, or simply hanging doors or heavy cabinets on the walls, they captivated me with their strength. Nothing was too heavy that some brawn or machinery couldn't move and manipulate into its desired position. Watching men lift heavy slabs of granite into place or hang huge chandeliers was something to marvel. Whatever I desired was the project manager's command, especially if the men got to use some muscle to provide it.

The men didn't seem to mind walking around in muddy work boots or hurling lumber, bricks, and shingles toward one another with their bare hands all while standing on high, shaky scaffolding. They didn't look bothered by standing in the scorching August sun or the freezing December rain. And eating outside with dirt-caked hands or using a porta potty stationed right by the road seemed as comfortable to them as it was awkward and stinky to me. They had no idea how much I was admiring and appreciating them day after day.

Just before the house was complete, I stood inside and watched two grown men as they squatted side by side at a sprinkler head trying to control its direction while squinting and laughing because they were being sprayed in the face with water. They may not have loved it, but they didn't seem fazed by it either. All through the building process, the men were on a mission to get the job done and they did it with grit, dirt, sweat, muscle, and masculine determination—especially if they knew a female was watching.

I thoroughly enjoyed watching the way the men used tools and machinery. It was quite entertaining! The looks on their faces when moving dirt around the lot with a Bobcat looked pretty much the same as the face of a little boy in a sandbox pretending to do the same with his plastic tractor.

So what was different about this experience compared to all the others? This experience was different because the *position of my heart was different*. I was seeing men through a new lens. I was seeing them the way God created them, through the keys of truth. This building project became a real-life laboratory experiment. By observing the men each day, it further solidified my already strong belief that *women need men*.

In all honesty, I think most women take men and their strength for granted. Imagine trying to build a home without men? Sure, it's possible, but it would take a whole lot more time and effort. You see, God designed men with a desire to work and make things with the strength of their muscles and the sweat of their brow. He wired men not only to want to prove but also provide through their masculinity.

It was during this same time that Don and I drove with Jonathan through Dallas/Fort Worth International Airport and saw construction crews working in a huge hole where a parking structure had once been. They were in the process of rebuilding it from below ground. I asked the guys, who were visually glued to the activity, "Do you see any women down there?" In unison, they responded, "Nope!"

There, among the rebar and concrete, were a lot of hard hats, and, not so surprisingly, they all belonged to men. Not one of the workers was female (as far as we could tell). When was the last time you drove by a roadside construction crew and saw a woman building a highway? How about building a skyscraper downtown?

WE NEED EACH OTHER

Down deep inside, women know they need men and men know they need women, but it's not socially acceptable to admit it aloud. If we were to go out on the street or eavesdrop on conversations in restaurants or coffee shops, how often do we hear women praising men or men praising women? Ladies, when was the last time you were standing in a group of females and they were speaking positively about men? And guys, when was the last time you were standing with a group of men and they were talking positively about confident, feminine women without any sexual connotations? Be honest, most of the time when one gender is talking about the other, our comments are *far* from positive. Men often think women are high maintenance and emotionally indulgent, and women think men are ignorant and not in touch with their feelings. (Something like that, right?) Could this be true even in church environments? I'm afraid it is. What do you think God thinks about that? Considering the Bible says "the Creator originally made man and woman for each other" (Matthew 19:4, MSG), I'm sure it makes Him very sad to see His kids with the opposite mindset. He knows it leaves us unprotected, lonely, and dare I say, incomplete.

Could it be that many cultures as well as the media, through magazines and advertisements, have adopted a negative attitude about the opposite gender? (If you don't believe me, just watch late night TV or some of the latest Hollywood blockbusters, and you'll begin to notice what they're saying about our roles. And the advertisements are just as bad! Once we start paying attention to these things, we'll become more sensitive to this truth.) Is it possible that at home and in the workplace, we have become more like adversaries than partners? Are we trustworthy toward one another or more focused on competing and working against one another? Is it all about winning for our specific gender? If so, why do you think that is?

Have things somehow been turned upside down and inside out? Whether you are married or single, the conflict is real. It's in our homes, offices, and yes, in some cases, even in churches and organizations that bear the name of Jesus. So how did we get here? What caused it, and how has it infiltrated the Bride of Christ, even if insidiously?

WARNING! Some of you, especially women, may not like or agree with what I am about to share, but if you keep reading, it may begin to make sense and bring you freedom and healing.

Let me share what I discovered in Dr. James Dobson's *Bringing Up Girls* (pp. 25–27):

> Boys are not at all like girls.... Between 1965 and 1995 ... some of the most highly educated and sophisticated people drew the conclusion that males and females were different only with regard to reproductive anatomy and physiology. The prevailing view was that every other distinguishing feature between the sexes had resulted from patriarchal upbringing. Boys, it was said, were coerced into being traditionally masculine, which was a serious problem for society. That belief, promoted with great passion by what was then called the Women's Liberation Movement, served to blind most psychiatrists, psychologists, neurologists, pediatricians, educators, politicians, writers, social activists, television personalities such as Phil Donahue and Barbara Walters, and millions of mothers and fathers throughout the Western world.... How could boys and girls be identical if their DNA is different?... The prevailing belief had been dead wrong.[2]

Many of us either were in school during those three decades or raised by parents who were. Because of this, I am simply suggesting we may have been more affected, both positively and negatively, by this movement than we may have realized.

FROM THE FATHER'S HEART

When Jesus rescued me from myself more than two decades ago, I began asking Him how we (the Church) got so far off from what He had so beautifully designed for us in the beginning. I have studied God's Word and been in ministry for more than 20 years and have been asking this question over and over again with no response. Then, about four years ago, God brought revelation when he gave me these keys of truth. With the revelation came a burden I believe is from the Father's heart, not just for me, but for the Church globally. The burden birthed passion to do something to help men and women find their way out of the fog.

So, what is the burden the Lord gave me?

- We have lost our way.

- Hollywood and the media in general are tools Satan is using to tear men and women apart and make us enemies.

- Men are being emasculated by women and by other men.

- Women are not being protected or covered by men because they have convinced men they don't need them.

- The word partner is more commonly used to describe homosexual relationships, rather than God-designed relationships between males and females.

- Gender confusion has reached an all-time high.

- Men and women compete and challenge one another instead of partnering and complementing one another.

Many women suffered much pain prior to and during the 1950s, which may have led to anger, rebellion, protests, movements, and the sexual revolution of the 1960s. "Bra burning," women refusing to take their husband's names, and songs with lyrics like "bringing home the bacon *and* frying it up in the pan" and "I am woman hear me roar" seem to have swung the pendulum of correction too far in the opposite direction. That pendulum was set in motion from the pain of women who had been unheard, disrespected, and underpaid. The pain was real, but the answers were often militant and demanding.

Emasculate
verb (used with object), emasculated, emasculating.
1. to castrate.
2. to deprive of strength or vigor; weaken.

adjective

3. deprived of or lacking strength or vigor; effeminate.[3]

So what have these movements taught us? Men, who were created by God to be hunters, warriors, and kings have, in many cases, lost their confidence, given up, and dropped their swords of defense for the females—wives, girlfriends, families, sisters, and friends—they could be protecting. These movements have also hurt young girls and women. Women are fearful, confused, and in many cases, full of pain and anger because they feel invisible, ignored, abandoned, and exposed. Women have picked up swords—sadly sometimes taking them away from the men who were created to protect them—and chosen to protect themselves and their children with a sword that was never fitted to them.

The organizers of these protests and movements genuinely hoped to bring freedom and to correct abuses, but instead often brought depression, destruction, and exhaustion among the women along with disunity between the sexes. The lies we believed from these movements have made us slaves and crippled both sexes. Women believed the lie that they have to force their way to be valued, cherished, and respected. The truth is the opposite has happened, and it's because when women try to force it, it causes men to feel confused and eventually pull away. It's not what either of us was built for and it's not in line with God's design. Damage has been done to more than one generation and will continue if we don't have the courage to take our God-designed positions with one another and speak truth.

Since the 1960s and the birth of feminism, the line of distinction between men and women continues to be blurred. Many are confused about what manhood and womanhood are; therefore, many parents don't know how to develop it in their children. Unfortunately, it was the misunderstanding that manhood is "to be above" womanhood that caused so much pain and pushed women to fight for feminism in the first place. Now we may have swung the pendulum too far in the other direction.

In her book, *Men and Women in the Church*, author Sarah Sumner explains this more:

> Secular feminists are keenly aware of the physical disparity that exists between women and men, but some don't like to talk about it for fear that any recognition of the difference between men's and women's strength will be used politically as an argument for male superiority. Thus they'd rather emphasize the common humanity of men and women. Evangelical feminists tend to have a similar point of view. As one Christian woman put it, "Men just so happen to be gendered as males, and women just so happen to be gendered as females. But basically, we're all just people."
>
> Another biblical feminist told me it's "un-strategic" to talk about the differences between men and women. She said that saying the word *different* ushers in a "death knell" to the global cause of women's concerns ....
>
> I can understand this woman's determination to be cautious. It is un-strategic politically for women to say that women are different from men. The problem is that when women are seen as different, men are seen as normal. The rationale flows like this:
>
> > Men are normal.
> >
> > Women are not men.
> >
> > Women are not normal.[4]

Freedom comes when we realize the truth and accept that men and women are different by design and complement one another. As contrary as it is to our current culture, women need men and men need women, and it's nothing to be ashamed of. Married and single women need men friends, co-workers, neighbors, and brothers in the faith, and married and single men need females in the same way. There are some things that are easier for men to do and some things that are easier for women to do. We are both human; we just have different strengths as males and females.

I was recently speaking at our church, and after the class, a man and woman approached me to talk about what they just heard. The man said, "Thank you so much for giving single men permission to be brothers to the single women in our group of friends. We see they need help, but they rarely let us help them, and we are afraid we will offend them if we ask." The woman next to him added, "We are afraid to look weak. We need to trust men more and let them know when we need their masculinity. I don't understand why we aren't comfortable with that."

Many women feel it's weak to let a man help them. Some even assume if they let men help that they will expect something in return. It's important for women to remember most men just want to show their abilities and strength because they are wired to do so. They aren't expecting anything from them.

GODLY SUBMISSION IN MARRIAGE

Instructions for Christian Households

Submit to one another out of reverence for Christ.

Wives, submit yourselves to your own husbands as you do to the Lord. For the husband is the head of the wife as Christ is the head of the church, his body, of which he is the Savior. Now as the church submits to Christ, so also wives should submit to their husbands in everything.

Husbands, love your wives, just as Christ loved the church and gave himself up for her to make her holy, cleansing her by the washing with water through the word, and to present her to himself as a radiant church, without stain

or wrinkle or any other blemish, but holy and blameless. In this same way, husbands ought to love their wives as their own bodies. He who loves his wife loves himself. After all, no one ever hated their own body, but they feed and care for their body, just as Christ does the church—for we are members of his body. "For this reason a man will leave his father and mother and be united to his wife, and the two will become one flesh." This is a profound mystery—but I am talking about Christ and the church. However, each one of you also must love his wife as he loves himself, and the wife must respect her husband.
Ephesians 5:21–33 (NIV)

Husbands and wives are called to "submit to one another," but we really don't like doing it, and it can become false submission when we try to force it. In most cases, it's because we really don't understand what godly submission is or how to do it authentically. (I know I had no idea!) Godly submission between a husband and wife brings power and security when they are submitted to God.

Submission
noun
1. an act or instance of submitting.
2. the condition of having submitted.
3. submissive conduct or attitude.[5]

Submission is the action or fact of accepting or yielding to a superior force or to the will or authority of another. When we submit to one another, we are *offering* ourselves and our gifts to them as a support,

> teammate, or partner. Submission is a form of respect
> and shows honor.

I believe our aversion to submission wasn't intentional, but more because we are all products of our environment. In some ways, all of us have inherited many of the beliefs we carry, even the ones we don't know we believe. Change can be hard, even when we are aching and begging for change. **So as you read through this book and discover portions you may not immediately relate to or accept, I beg you to *pause, ponder, pray,* and *obey.*** My prayer is that just like me, you will find freedom from the pages of this book. All you need to do is open your heart and ask God to give you the eyes to see and the understanding you need.

As we dig deeper and take a closer look at the keys about men and women, it's important to remember I'm sharing keys of truth for *emotionally healthy people*, not perfect people. The World Health Organization describes mental health as "a state of well-being in which the individual realizes his or her own abilities, can cope with the normal stresses of life, can work productively and fruitfully, and is able to make a contribution to his or her community."[6] If I could add to that, I'd say to be whole you *must* also be born again and have a teachable heart yielded to the Holy Spirit.

There are also people who are wounded and broken because of their environments or personal choices. In some cases, these individuals may *not* be healthy. Unhealthy people can become *abusive* and manipulative, because they have a warped sense of God's design. No one should use the keys of truth found in this book as a reason to stay in an abusive situation. Please, if you're not sure, seek godly, professional counsel and help.

PAUSE, PONDER, PRAY, AND OBEY

MEN

- Will you admit God designed you to need women in your life?

- Are you getting what you need from the women in your life? If not, why do you think this is?

- Is there distance between you and someone you are supposed to be partnering with? If so, why and what can you do to change it?

- What in your past or current environment has formed or shaped you that goes against God's original plan?

  - If it is a person, think of them now.

  - Can you understand how it happened?

  - Can you forgive them? If you are willing, ask God to help you forgive them.

WOMEN

- Will you admit God designed you to need men in your life?

- Are you getting what you need from the men in your life? If not, why do you think that is?

- Is there distance between you and someone you are supposed to be partnering with? If so, why and what can you do to change it?

- What in your past or current environment has formed or shaped you that goes against God's original plan?

  - If it is a person, think of them now.

  - Can you understand how it happened?

  - Can you forgive them? If you are willing, ask God to help you forgive them.

What is the Holy Spirit saying to you? Take some time to find three scripture verses that encourage you or confirm what you are hearing. (You may begin by looking up a word related to this chapter in the concordance in the back of your Bible.)

_____

_____

_____

_____

_____

_____

_____

_____

_____

_____

_____

_____

The world is unprincipled. It's dog-eat-dog out there! The world doesn't fight fair. But we don't live or fight our battles that way—never have and never will. The tools of our trade aren't for marketing or manipulation, but they are for demolishing that entire massively corrupt culture. We use our powerful God-tools for smashing warped philosophies, tearing down barriers erected against the truth of God, fitting every loose through and emotion and impulse into the structure of life shaped by Christ. Our tools are ready at hand for clearing the ground of every obstruction and building lives of obedience into maturity.
2 Corinthians 10:3–6 (MSG)

Chapter 3

DIFFERENT BY DESIGN

As a child, if our son, Jonathan, saw a cord laying on the floor, he would try to find a place to plug it in. If he was outside, he might use it as a rope to tie a skateboard to his trike with one of his sister's stuffed animals strapped on top, giving it the ride of its life! If he discovered a tool, he would find a way to use it. If he found an empty box, he would kick it, step on it, or stand on it, trying to test its durability to see what kind of pressure it took to crush it. Sometimes, he'd use it as a stool to stand on as he guarded his kingdom from enemy attack in his imaginary battle.

On the other hand, if our daughter, Holly, found an empty box, she would carry it around the house looking for items to put inside of it, such as a small stuffed animal or doll. She would thoughtfully arrange the objects inside the box and carefully place the lid securely on top so nothing would fall out. Sometimes she collected rocks she thought were beautiful, flowers from the garden she felt were too pretty to stay outside, or lost, lonely rollie pollies who needed a home. (She really did love them. *Yuck!*) Whatever ended up inside that box was her treasure. To her, they were precious things she'd collected and cared about.

As you can see, their responses were vastly different, and it's because God made them different by design. When we take time to observe children, it's easy to see God's design inherent in little boys and girls from the time they are born.

We should recognize that at every age there are some very obvious and somewhat extreme physical differences between males and females, and these differences were built into each gender for a purpose.

The next time you're around the opposite gender, take a close look. Do their hands, shoulders, and arms look different from yours? Is the texture of their skin and hair different from yours? Even science has proven that male and female brains are different.[7, 8] A woman may be taller than a man, but most likely she would not be able to overpower him because his muscle mass and bone density is so much stronger than hers. Also, while most women are strong verbally and emotionally, most men are physically stronger because of the differences in their physical composition. Women don't have the same testosterone levels as men, which make his muscles and bones different from female muscles and bones. No matter how hard women may try, they just don't have the cell structure, muscle mass, bone density, or skin texture to do what men were designed to do.[9] And, on the flip side, no matter how much a woman might wish a man could experience ovulation, a menstrual cycle, or even child birth, he can't! We were created different by design.We were created different *for* one another.

For God does not show favoritism.
Romans 2:11 (NIV)

GOD'S ORIGINAL DESIGN

The first step to understanding God's design for the sexes is to see how He created us from the beginning. So, let's see what the Creator of the Universe had in mind when he designed men and women.

Once the earth was stable enough to sustain life, "God said, 'Let Us make man in Our image, according to Our likeness; let them have dominion over ... every living thing that moves on the earth'" (Genesis 1:26–28, NKJV). Notice that He did *not* say, "Let males have dominion over females," yet this is what many people think the Bible says. Healthy, godly men do not want to dominate women; they want to partner with them. Then, in Genesis 2:7, 18–23 (NLT) we read that, "The Lord God formed the man from the dust of the ground. He breathed the breath of life into the man's nostrils, and the man became a living person. The Lord God said, 'It is not good for the man to be alone. I will make a helper who is just right for him.' So the Lord God formed from the ground all the wild animals and all the birds of the sky. He brought them to the man to see what he would call them, and the man chose a name for each one ... but still there was no helper just right for him. So the Lord God caused the man to fall into a deep sleep. While the man slept, the Lord God took out one of the man's ribs and closed up the opening. Then the Lord God made a woman from the rib, and he brought her to the man. 'At last!' the man exclaimed. 'This one is bone from my bone, and flesh from my flesh! She will be called "woman," because she was taken from "man."'"

After God the Father made Adam out of dust of the ground,

He breathed into Adam's nostrils and gave him life; he recognized Adam needed a helper suitable for him. So out of the *same* ground He used to form Adam, God made all of the livestock, birds of the air, and beasts of the field. Yet *even though* they were created out of the same ground as Adam, *he didn't find a companion.* It's interesting that even though Adam was in the presence of God, he still needed a companion. He needed a woman! Christians often say, "God is enough. I don't need a wife. Or I don't need a husband." Yet I find it curious that God knew that even in His presence Adam needed someone else, a helpmate. If you're single, please hear my heart. I am not suggesting being single is less than desirable; my point is *we were designed to need the opposite gender.* God knew man needed woman! When God said it wasn't good for man to be alone, he wasn't saying man was bad or evil, he was simply acknowledging that man needed "a helper who is just right for him." God made things "good" for Adam and provided for his need by giving him a woman.

Could it be God let Adam feel a need and a desire so He could create something for him and have the pleasure of giving her to him as a gift, a token of His love and affection for Adam? We know from His Word He is a giver, not a *taker.* God may have wanted to show Adam *more* proof of his *amazing creativity.* **The companion God made for Adam was not made from his head to rule over him or from his feet to be walked on by him, but from his side to walk safely beside him and under his arm of protection and provision.** And isn't it interesting that God put Adam in a deep sleep, so he would not see his bride until she was *delivered* to him? God wanted to deliver Eve to Adam as a gift, not a possession. She was to be as a queen, not a slave.

Do you think God had planned to give Eve to Adam all along? He may have wanted this recorded so that men and women would realize, even from the beginning, He loves to give us the desires of our hearts (Psalm 20:4; Psalm 37:4). While the Bible doesn't say Adam verbally asked for Eve, maybe the Lord wanted to let Adam *feel the desire* so he would be ready to *receive* her as a precious treasure.

We see a beautiful representation of this in Christian weddings today. The bride is escorted down the aisle by her father (or by someone who is also standing in for her heavenly Father). She willfully gives herself (submits all she is and all she has) to the bridegroom. The expectant bridegroom waits to receive her as a gift and is filled with joy and awe because he's looking at something God has made just for him coming down the aisle. When a bride and groom do things in God's order, something supernatural happens in the ceremony. **I believe our Heavenly Father delights in giving a bride to a bridegroom because it is a picture of what He longs to do for Jesus when He is united with His bride.** Jesus is in heaven today waiting for the Father to say, "Son, go get your bride." When the bridegroom has not taken the bride before she has been given to him, God is delighted and His presence fills the atmosphere.

TODAY'S CULTURE SUGGESTS THE OPPOSITE

Sadly, our culture suggests that men should do the opposite. If a man wants a woman, he should take her, even if she is not his. Instead of men covering and protecting women from making mistakes that can lead to unwanted pregnancies, single parenting, sexually transmitted diseases, abortions, brokenness, rejection, loneliness, and many other things, they are "taking" women as their own. And the message for women in today's culture isn't any better. Too many women discount their value and worth by giving themselves away (body and soul) before they're married. The problem with that is we don't belong to ourselves; *we belong to God.* 1 Corinthians 6:19–20 (NLT) says, "Don't you realize that your body is the temple of the Holy Spirit, who lives in you and was given to you by God? You do not belong to yourself, for God bought you with a high price. So you must honor God with your body." Women are designed to desire provision and protection and ache to be desired and cherished. It usually isn't hard to take advantage of women who have a God-designed need that hasn't been met yet; it is hard to be unselfish and exercise self-control.

To God, any kind of sex outside of marriage is not okay, because it damages the hearts of men and women with long-term consequences, whether they realize it or not at the time. (I once heard, you can choose your sin, but you can't choose your consequences.) In many cases, women are giving themselves to men because they are desperate for provision and protection. For many, yes even Christians, it seems normal to live together and play house. They justify it by saying it's providing a jumpstart to the marriage—it's less expensive to live together and it's a way to test the waters of the relationship. Yet, statistics prove that in the end it can be deadly to the marriage.[10] I also believe it creates a dangerous appetite for sexual intimacy outside of marriage.

In addition to this, some women become self-sufficient and, out of fear, try to appear stronger than they really are. Many women today believe it's weak to need a man, so they pretend they don't need or want one and try to force themselves into something they were not designed to do or be. Women who have bought into this lie are exhausted. The truth is women's physical bodies were not designed to carry that kind of emotional and physical weight. When women try to battle and war like a man, it causes confusion and nonverbally signals strong men to stay away. Yet many women feel if they don't prove their strength and keep up the façade, men will take advantage of them. Women who have been hurt by men or believe they don't need a man may think it's safer to take advantage of a man before he takes advantage of them. All of these are lies from the pit of hell and break God's heart because it goes against His original plan.

The current world's system, coupled with our humanity,

seems to make adversarial relationships between men and women feel normal, but they aren't. However, the more we understand and accept our gender differences and how they are carefully distributed by God, the more stable, healthy, and fulfilling our relationships can be. **God put a longing and desire into women for men, and men were built to be what women need. It's God's design.**

I have met many women who are on a mission to change the men in their lives to become the men *they want* them to be. It's important for women to understand they probably can't change men, but they can change the way they view them, which is a great place to begin. A woman's behavior toward a man might just change the way he sees her and responds to her. Men never feel as strong as when they're positioned to protect the women in their lives, but this can only happen when women take their positions and allow men to take theirs.

• • •

We recently attended a wedding, and when the back doors of the chapel opened, the bride and her father entered the doorway and began to make their way down the aisle. Every eye was on her, and she seemed uncomfortable with the attention all being on her. Someone suggested to her before the wedding that if she could get close enough to lock eyes with her groom, everyone else would fade away. It was a beautiful thing to witness as their eyes met and the faint smile on her face became a look of complete contentment. Almost without blinking, she continued down the aisle holding tightly to her daddy's arm.

What happened next was a shock to everyone. As she moved closer to her waiting groom at the front of the church, *he* broke down and began to weep. Bending at the waist, with one hand over his face and the other in his pant pocket, he began to cry. I don't believe there was a dry eye in the room as the Spirit of God entered in and made His presence known. *The groom was so grateful for this beautiful gift approaching him that he could not contain his emotion.*

I was once again reminded of what God initiated in the Garden of Eden all those years ago. God put Adam to sleep while He fashioned Eve and *then* presented her to Adam as a gift. In a Christian marriage, this symbolizes God delivering a bride to her groom. She is a gift for the groom to cherish, provide for, and protect *for God.* When a couple honors God by not taking one another physically until they've made a covenant with Him, I believe God is anxious to come and be the master of the ceremony. When we do things in the wrong order or get things upside down, we are the ones that lose the preciousness of the gift God is giving emotionally, physically, and spiritually. God wants us to have the best He has to offer—*a spouse as a holy gift from Him.* If you have gotten this backward, know that you can trust in God, believing He is gracious, and repent. There is no condemnation in Christ Jesus! We all can get a fresh start and a new slate when we yield, repent, and ask Him to restore us.

There is therefore now no condemnation to those who are in Christ Jesus, who do not walk according to the flesh,

but according to the Spirit. For the law of the Spirit of life in Christ Jesus has made me free from the law of sin and death. For what the law could not do in that it was weak through the flesh, God did by sending His own Son in the likeness of sinful flesh, on account of sin: He condemned sin in the flesh, that the righteous requirement of the law might be fulfilled in us who do not walk according to the flesh but according to the Spirit. For those who live according to the flesh set their minds on the things of the flesh, but those who live according to the Spirit, the things of the Spirit. For to be carnally minded is death, but to be spiritually minded is life and peace. Because the carnal mind is enmity against God; for it is not subject to the law of God, nor indeed can be. So then, those who are in the flesh cannot please God. But you are not in the flesh but in the Spirit, if indeed the Spirit of God dwells in you. Now if anyone does not have the Spirit of Christ, he is not His. And if Christ is in you, the body is dead because of sin, but the Spirit is life because of righteousness. But if the Spirit of Him who raised Jesus from the dead dwells in you, He who raised Christ from the dead will also give life to your mortal bodies through His Spirit who dwells in you.
Romans 8:1–11 (NKJV)

DIFFERENT ON PURPOSE

Most of us have not considered our differences are on purpose. They're not a curse. God created us all with uniqueness, and He wants to use these differences in our lives and the lives of others. God uses our differences as tools for our sanctification to make us *holy* and *whole*. We each bring into the relationship what the other one lacks. And it's through the Holy Spirit and our relationships with one another that we are sanctified. "But you were washed, but you were sanctified, but you were justified in the name of the Lord Jesus and by the Spirit of our God" (1 Corinthians 1:11, NKJV).

There are general attitudes about our lives, good and bad, which come from our upbringings. Our environments influence us all. The people who raised us influenced and affected our views of our masculinity and femininity as well as the way we view the opposite gender. Personal history or present situations may make it hard for some to believe men were originally wired with a default to love women and women were wired to love men. I'm here to tell you God's plan and purpose for Adam and Eve is still in place today. God does not change his mind, and nothing is going to change God's plan. Women will always need men and men will always need women.

At this point, **some of you may be thinking, I'm different. I don't fit into the male or female definitions described so far. Please keep reading! God is much too creative to make each of us exactly alike.** The focus is on God's original purpose and position for males and females that started in the Garden of Eden. The goal here is to consider the overall differences between males and females to reveal the truth about God's design.

In our culture, it seems as though men have become prejudice toward women and women have become prejudice against men. Meaning we "pre-judge" each other. It's time to expose and break the bonds of confusion the enemy has tied to us and to our culture. Don't let stereotypes and pre-judgments confuse you or trip you up. Just stay open and listen to what the Holy Spirit is saying to you, because it may bring healing and clear up misunderstandings you may hold without realizing it.

As we continue this journey, take a moment and ask God to show you what He wants you to see and learn about yourself *and* the opposite gender.

Are you ready to begin? Here we go!

DISTINCTIONS BETWEEN MEN AND WOMEN

	MALE	FEMALE
Functions	**Provider** (Hunter)	**Collector** (Beautifier)
	Protector (Warrior)	**Connector** (Nurturer)
	Leader (King)	**Comforter** (Queen)
Compositions	**Dirt/Refined Rock** (Solid)	**Bone and Flesh** (Fluid)
Emotional Operations	**Telescope**	**Radar**
Symbols	**Ceramic Coffee Mug**	**Crystal Pitcher**
Core Needs	**Honor** and **Respect**	**Provision** and **Protection**

MALE AND FEMALE FUNCTIONS

MEN ARE DESIGNED BY GOD TO BE PROVIDERS (HUNTERS), PROTECTORS (WARRIORS), AND LEADERS (KINGS)

When was the last time you sat on a bench at a mall, playground, school, or church and just observed little boys? *They're fascinating!* Boys are wired for adventure. If you take the time, you'll see that from the moment they can walk they're becoming hunters, warriors, and kings. They demonstrate their unique maleness by trying to provide, protect, and lead. A boy will make a sword or a weapon of some kind out of a stick, empty wrapping paper roll, or even his finger (if that's all he has available). Then he'll look for something or someone to protect or conquer. He'll scan the horizon, looking for a brick wall or tree stump—anything he can climb—not only to prove he can, but also to show his strength. Boys are relentlessly looking for ways to demonstrate their power and ability, if only to their mothers. From playing king of the mountain on the jungle gym to proudly bringing bugs, frogs, or crawfish home to mom as part of the bounty from their victories, they look for opportunities to battle, conquer, climb, and compete.

Ladies, when you look at the men in your life, consider this: There is *always* a little boy full of adventure inside of them. Wives, inside the man you married is a little boy who would still climb the highest mountain and scrape up his knees, his elbows, and his hands until they were bruised and bloodied just to get to the top to prove to you he is worthy of your respect and affection. He's designed to show you his masculinity, and he'll never outgrow it. This God-given need is there to make *you* feel secure.

WOMEN ARE DESIGNED BY GOD TO BE COLLECTORS (BEAUTIFIERS), CONNECTORS (NURTURERS), AND SUPPORTERS (QUEENS)

Even as toddlers, little girls play house with their baby dolls by dressing them up, taking care of them, teaching them at imaginary school, and making sure they feel cared for and loved. A little girl loves playing dress up with her mommy's shoes, jewelry, and clothes, especially when she gets to wear flowing garments that billow as she twirls. These beautiful, little creatures come out of the womb looking for ways to collect and connect with people, places, and things. A little girl's desire to be cherished and cared for is connected to the healthy affection of her daddy. She longs to see the delight in his eyes as she gracefully curtseys in front of him. He is her prince and his ability to make her feel his love, approval, and protection is vital to her self-esteem as she matures into a woman. Little girls are wired by God to look for their prince as provider and protector. Girls look to their fathers (or other male figures) to fill this role.

Men, when you look at a woman, consider this: There is *always* a little girl who desires to be told she's beautiful and valued. That same little girl who played dress up with her mommy's clothes is the one who now gets dressed up for you and asks you how she looks. She values your opinion because she has a desire to please you. She's designed to connect with you, and she'll never outgrow it. This God-given need is there to make *you* feel secure too.

Some of you may be like me. In the beginning of this process, I thought, *I am more like a man in some ways. I'm independent and strong.* Maybe you're thinking the same thing right now. In some ways, you may feel you've switched roles. Based on my experience, if I had to guess, I'd say approximately 20 percent of men behave more like women and 20 percent of women behave more like men. The reasons for this could be their upbringing or the environment they grew up in. Twenty percent of the men may be more emotional and communicative, and 20 percent of the women may be more focused, direct, and take-charge than her female counterparts. It's not wrong; it's just not the norm. In this book, I am addressing 80 percent of the general population of each gender to help us better understand one another and give each other grace. If you don't fit into the exact descriptions, please keep reading because it might help clear up some confusion. I hope to bring awareness of what has been going on in American culture these past five decades while helping both genders understand and embrace their wiring. I hope to bring value for one another and help us thrive as we do life together as friends, family members, and co-workers.

Being raised in the '60s and '70s by parents of that era had caused more confusion for me than I realized. I am not talking about sexual orientation or addressing any degree of gender confusion here. There are boys who are artistic and creative, but they do these things in a masculine way because their masculinity has been called forth and developed. There are girls who are athletes or tomboys who may not be what some call a "girly girl," but their femininity is fully developed and intact. The genetic makeup of both boys and girls and the environments they are raised in make a difference in how they develop, see, and express themselves. **God's creative enough to make us all specifically individual, but He has a plan and position in mind for both genders and it's there to bring order.**

● ● ●

Growing up, I was a tomboy and was proud of it! One of my favorite things to do was go out on the boat with my dad. He was an airline pilot and often had weekdays off, which gave us the opportunity to go out to the lake on days it wasn't as crowded. On one particular day, there weren't any other boats out on the lake and the water was as smooth as glass. Once we got the boat out to the center of the lake, my dad threw his ski into the water, followed by a rope, and then he jumped in. "You're going to pull me," he shouted up to me. I had driven the boat often, but to drive it solo with no one else in the boat to spot me while pulling him on the ski was horrifying! Not to mention I was only 11! Doubting my abilities, questions flooded my mind. *What if I run over him when it's time to circle around and pick him up? What if he falls? What if he gets hurt?* I was terrified, but I did it! The whole time my dad kept saying, "Would I ask you to do anything I don't know you *can* do?" He had more faith in me than I had in myself. From that point forward, I drove the boat and trailered it with ease. I even learned how to pull off boat motors and rebuild them on the boat dock with my dad's help. And it wasn't long before I knew every tool in his garage. (I prided myself in knowing how to use them!) I *loved* doing things most people more closely associate with boys' activities and was pretty proud of it!

I continued to go to the lake alone to ski and play—the only thing I needed was a guy to help me manually lift the heavy outboard motor up and back the trailer in when we were pulling the boat out of the water. My dad felt it was important for me, as a female, to be independent and strong and, evidently, I did too.

MALE AND FEMALE COMPOSITIONS

GOD DESIGNED THE MALE COMPOSITION AS SOLID

Solid: A definite shape or volume not a liquid or gas; firm or compact in substance; not hollow; has the same substance or color throughout; continuous; substantial and hearty; upstanding and dependable.

I find it very interesting that God could create the first human being out of anything but He chose to make Adam, the first human on planet earth, from *dirt*, which is refined rock. (Guys, if you think about it, that's not a bad thing. Without dirt, seed will never grow. You are foundationally and fundamentally important!) You may have even heard someone say, "That man is solid as a rock." That's because *most* men are more rugged and less emotional than women are. Science recognizes and acknowledges that the male is the physically stronger of the two genders. Men's testosterone levels bring abundant strength and physical differences. Men are created with a completely different *skill set* than women. Men have grit and strength and are not afraid to get sweaty or dirty. They have a built-in need for adventure, exploration, and competition. Most men enjoy being outside hunting, boating, golfing, camping, playing sports, or competing in some way.

GOD DESIGNED THE FEMALE COMPOSITION AS FLUID

Fluid: Flows freely, like water; often used to describe something that can change easily or often; adaptable; has particles that easily move and change their perspective or position without separation of the mass that easily yields to pressure; is subject to change or movement.

A female's fluidity is often what frustrates men most about women. Her *fluidity* can best be described as water flowing down a mountain into a stream that works its way around boulders, plants, and debris. Instead of letting the boulders and rocks stop her, she adjusts and makes her way around them. A woman's fluidity, along with her ability to adapt, collect, and connect, is what allows her to be the glue that holds families and relationships together, both at home and at the office.

I find it interesting that the first female on planet earth was not made from *dirt* but was fashioned from man's rib. She was composed of Adam's *bone* and *flesh*. Let's look at what that symbolizes.

Bone is the *rigid connective tissue* that makes up the skeleton, while flesh is the *soft connective tissue* of the body that holds it together. Is it any wonder that the Lord would use both rigid and soft connective tissue to make the first female? Women naturally bring and hold people, places, and things together spiritually and emotionally. Like *bone*, when a woman is healthy emotionally and physically, she can bend before she breaks. But when women are not nurtured, nourished, provided for, and protected, they can become brittle and easily snap into pieces, and oftentimes when they do, everything falls apart.

The *flesh* represents the *soft tissue*, which is also symbolic of a woman's fluidity, tenderness, adaptability, and sensitivity to the people and things going on around her. Females are wired by God to collect, connect, and bring order. The males in a female's life are fortunate to have her skill set, which is very different from theirs. Men innately know they need women, and these explanations usually help men understand more about *why* that need is there.

MALE AND FEMALE OPERATIONS

GOD CREATED THE MALE EMOTIONAL OPERATION TO WORK LIKE A TELESCOPE

Most males are single-focused and, much like a telescope, can only focus on one thing at a time. It's not easy for men to be doing one thing and immediately switch and be completely engaged in something else. If a man is cleaning the garage, his focus is on *cleaning the garage*. If he is watching sports, *he is watching sports*. When a man's driving a car it's often difficult for him to have an intimate conversation because his focus is on driving and arriving to his destination on time without getting lost or asking for directions. (Remember, he has to prove he is a warrior and a hunter.) Men can only *fully* engage in one thing at a time.

Ladies, it may be freeing to know a man cannot focus on two things at once; therefore, he cannot choose to watch the game and ignore you at the same time.

GOD CREATED THE FEMALE EMOTIONAL OPERATION
TO WORK LIKE A RADAR

Maybe it is because of her fluidity, but most of us know women are multitaskers and multifaceted. It seems as though women have a built-in radar that allows them to sense danger, collect and connect to beauty, and see the needs of the people around them—sometimes all at one time. A woman is constantly aware of what is going on around her within a certain radius. A female's radar is not usually off unless she is asleep. (Even then, she's usually the first to hear a child cry.) Her radar is not just of great value to her, but also to those in her life, both at home and work.

MALE & FEMALE SYMBOLS

GOD MADE MALES LIKE CERAMIC COFFEE MUGS

When creating a clay mug, a potter begins by placing a large, damp lump of clay (dirt) onto a potter's wheel. As the lump of cold, wet clay turns on the spinning wheel, the potter begins to form the outer shape by applying pressure from the outside. After a few minutes, the potter begins to apply pressure to the inside by forcing his hand down into the lump of clay. Constantly dipping his hands in water to keep the clay wet, he begins to apply balanced pressure from the inside out, which creates a void, or a hole, in the vessel. Once the mug is finished and allowed to dry, it is dipped and fired in an intensely hot kiln, which makes it strong and resilient. Now it is a hollow vessel, ready for service.

Have you ever noticed a mug doesn't have sections or dividers? A mug, by design, can only hold *one thing* at a time. It's cylindrical in shape and has a handle. It's solid, durable, and rugged. Glazed and fired for strength, a clay mug is not translucent and can withstand heat, pressure, and sudden jolts. It may chip, but it rarely shatters. It does not have a spout for pouring or a hole in the bottom for draining. It has one purpose—to *hold one* thing at a time.

Like clay mugs, men can only hold (focus on) one thing at a time. They are strong, insulated, durable, functional, and unembellished. Men are physically and functionally solid, strong, rugged, and formed from dirt (clay). Isaiah 64:8 (NIV) says, "Yet you, Lord, are our Father. We are the clay, you are the potter; we are all the work of your hand." Isn't it interesting that when making a mug, the clay must be hollow before the potter can fill it? In the same way, a man must be filled by the Holy Spirit before he can truly fulfill the purpose he was created for.

GOD MADE FEMALES LIKE CRYSTAL PITCHERS

It's just as fascinating to look at the making of a crystal pitcher. What makes a crystal pitcher different from a glass pitcher is the lead that's added to the glass to make it more clear, pure, radiant, and less of a blue/green color. The lead crystal is subjected to intense heat in a furnace and at the perfect time, the molten—or heat-softened glass—is held at the end of a blowpipe (a hollow, stainless steel tube) and a master glassblower *blows his own* breath into it with precise pressure and speed, turning it with slow precision. (Isn't it interesting that breath is what's used to hollow out the glass and make it ready to serve?) The glassblower then uses a marver to cool and shape the molten glass. As the glass begins to form the shape of a pitcher, he then places the glass handle on the side. Next, the glassblower uses water and a circular saw to cut ridges into the pitcher. This complex process requires the perfect angle and a balanced design. Cutting ridges into the pitcher adds character to the design and produces a colorful prismatic effect. When the light passes through the pitcher at different angles, the light refracts and separates into a visible spectrum, creating a beautiful and colorful rainbow. Just as the potter applies pressure in the development stage of the clay mug, the artist applies pressure with a saw into the crystal to create indentions and cuts to cause the reflection of light to benefit the piece, bringing beauty and color. Once the design is complete, the master can use the crystal pitcher to pour liquid into a vessel of his choosing.

So often, we, as women, don't like the pressure or the pain of deep cuts, but when done by a Master artist, the cuts are worth enduring because they bring uniqueness and beauty that reflect the creativity and glory of the Master who made them.

Crystal pitchers are fragile and delicate. The smallest jolt or the slightest sudden pressure of a sharp angle can cause them to shatter. They are clear and transparent; you can easily see what's inside and if they're clean or dirty. Their deep cuts and ridges refract light and become more beautiful when they're in the light. In the same way, women only display true beauty when they are in the Light. Women must allow Light to pierce their hearts and bounce in and out in order for their color and sparkle to be a benefit.

MALE AND FEMALE CORE NEEDS

GOD CREATED MALES TO NEED HONOR AND RESPECT

God created males with a core need to be honored and respected, but the amazing revelation is **a man's ability to feel honored and respected may be directly attached to his ability to provide for and protect the females in his life.** God wired men to have a need to be recognized and appreciated for their value and worth, so when allowed to provide and protect, they feel honor and respect. Many times the men in our culture feel disrespected and dishonored because the women in their lives do not allow them to protect and provide for them, which emasculates men and strips them of their purpose.

●●●

Due to pressures in today's culture, many women are in self-preservation mode and say things like, "I can do this myself." Or "I don't need a man to complete me!" It's because they have believed lies about themselves and men. This type of behavior is harmful to women and emasculating to men. It creates confusion, and eventually men react by disengaging or shutting down altogether. No matter how strong men may seem or how confident they are, deep down inside they need to know they are valued by the women who depend upon them. And women need to know men can be depended upon.

GOD CREATED FEMALES TO NEED PROVISION AND PROTECTION

We have all heard that women need security, which is true. **But what if a female can't feel entirely secure unless she is provided for and protected (emotionally, spiritually, and physically) by a male or males?** Women need to feel secure, nurtured, and cherished by the men in their lives (fathers, husbands, friends, etc.). This kind of security is what makes a woman *thrive*. **Women want respect too, but the reasons are different. Her need for respect is often related to her need to be cherished and safe.**

MADE FOR EACH OTHER

The bottom line is men are wired to provide and protect and can only feel **honored** and **respected** when they are able to do so for the women in their life. Women are wired to **need provision** and **protection** that only men can give. **God created women to**

need what men *need* to give. So it's true, God did design us to need what only the other gender can provide. No matter how we try to stretch or change it, His way and plan will forever be true. He made us different on purpose. He made us *for* each other, not to work against one another. **God's plan is simple yet *brilliant*!**

PAUSE, PONDER, PRAY, AND OBEY

MEN

1. What were you designed to do?
2. What were you designed to need?
3. Do you believe that?
4. Will you embrace your strengths and your differences?
5. Are you willing to observe both genders, young and old, for the next week and see if the distinctions are true?
6. When was the last time you saw the little girl in your wife, girlfriend, friends, or co-workers? Ask the Lord to show you what He sees when He looks at the girls and women in your world.
7. What do they need?
8. Are you able and willing to give it? If not, why not?
9. Is pain there? How does that make you feel?

WOMEN

1. What were you designed to do?
2. What were you designed to need?
3. Do you believe that?
4. Will you embrace your strengths and your differences?
5. Are you willing to observe both genders, young and old, for the next week and see if the distinctions are true?

6. When was the last time you looked for the little boy in your husband, boyfriend, friends, or co-workers? Ask the Lord to show you what He sees when He looks at the boys and men in your world.

7. What do they need?

8. Are you able and willing to give it? If not, why not?

9. Are you willing to allow men to provide for and protect you? If not, why not?

10. Is pain there? How does that make you feel?

But we are bound to give thanks to God always for you, brethren beloved by the Lord, because God from the beginning chose you for salvation through sanctification by the Spirit and belief in the truth, to which He called you by our gospel, for the obtaining of the glory of our Lord Jesus Christ.
2 Thessalonians 2:13–14 (NKJV)

What is the Holy Spirit saying to you? Take some time to find three scripture verses that encourage you or confirm what you are hearing.

_____

_____

_____

_____

_____

_____

_____

_____

_____

_____

_____

_____

_____

_____

_____

_____

_____

_____

_____

_____

_____

_____

_____

_____

_____

_____

_____

_____

_____

_____

_____

_____

_____

I pray that out of His glorious riches he may strengthen you with power through His Spirit in your inner being, so that Christ may dwell in your hearts through faith. And I pray that you, being rooted and established in love, may have power, together with all the Lord's holy people, to grasp how wide and long and high and deep is the love of Christ, and to know this love that surpasses knowledge—that you may be filled to the measure of all the fullness of God. Now to him who is able to do immeasurably more than all we can ask or imagine, according to his power that is at work within us, to him be glory in the church and in Christ Jesus throughout all generations, for ever and ever! Amen.
Ephesians 3:16–21 (NIV)

Chapter 4

DIFFERENT FOR A PURPOSE

Now that it's clear males and females are made differently and intended for different positions, we are going to look at how God uses the opposite gender as tools in His hands to sanctify us—to make us holy and transform us into the likeness of Christ. Sanctification only comes when in relationship with each other and with Christ. Oftentimes, the Holy Spirit uses marriage as a means of sanctification. **Yet, amazingly, we don't have to be married for the Lord to use the opposite gender to sanctify us; our differences are built in us to help us and teach us.**

Sanctify them by Your truth. Your word is truth. As You sent Me into the world, I also have sent them into the world.
John 17:17–18 (NKJV)

Men are born to be warriors, hunters, and kings. By nature, men are not nurturers or tender shepherds, but through the sanctification process, they can become more like Christ, wielding a sword of protection in one hand and nurturing as a tender shepherd with the other. The more men have the character and attributes of Christ, the more natural the nurturing and tenderness becomes.

Women are by nature beautifiers, nurturers, and queens. Most women find it easy to nurture; however, in today's world, it's not so natural for her to drop her sword and stop providing for and protecting herself and those she loves. **For a woman, the sanctification process is learning to trust, yield to Christ, and believe that God will position men in her life who will provide for and protect her. She must learn to trust the men God has placed in her life and lay down her sword of self-protection and defense.**

A woman collects information and connects with people, places, and things all day, every day. She goes to work, enjoys friends, runs errands, and takes kids to school. In other words, a woman is all over the place—her radar is on and her list is endless. At the end of her day, it's important she has the opportunity to "pour out" what she's collected in her soul (pitcher) all day. A man can offer her help by learning to gently "hold her handle" and let her *pour*—this in turn makes more room for him. There's another benefit: This daily exercise brings an opportunity for *his sanctification.* This practice helps him become more like Jesus—a humble and tender shepherd. As women drop their swords, it encourages men to take their positions as providers, protectors, and leaders.

Men, God doesn't want you to lay down your swords or cease to be hunters and warriors. This is what you were created to be. He doesn't want to strip you of your masculinity. But what He does want is for you to be a sanctified warrior with the heart of a tender, nurturing shepherd.

Women, God doesn't want you to cease collecting,

connecting, nurturing, and beautifying. That's what he created you to do, but He wants you to stop being your own provider and protector. He wants you to make room for a man, a tender shepherd, who will step in and cover you. (This could be a husband, friend, brother, or any other man who is willing to fill this role.)

THE ZIPPER EFFECT

Let's look again at the first man and woman. When we learn the needs of both genders and begin to understand their wiring, we can't help but see that *we were designed to balance one another out.* When we take our different positions and align them with one another, we fit together like a zipper. I like to call this the "zipper effect." Everyone knows what a zipper looks like, but it's worth noting that a zipper has a slider that either interlocks or separates the toothed tracks when pulled. Like a zipper, we can interlock with each other to bring supernatural unity and support, which also gives us the ability to keep the enemy out of our relationships. When we are not partnering with the Lord and each other, we're being pulled and separated. Satan is the author of confusion, and his plan is to convince us to be *more alike so we don't need one another or, even worse, to be adversaries.* But nothing could be further from the truth. **God's original plan will not be reordered by what any society thinks or suggests. *Culture does not determine our truth.* When we take our positions and interlock with the Lord and each other, we become unified. We fit together, like a zipper, locking out the enemy and his lies.**

After Satan targeted the weakness and selfishness of Adam and Eve and provided them with the opportunity to sin, "The Lord God said to the serpent: 'Because you have done this, you are cursed more than all cattle, and more than every beast of the field; on your belly you shall go, and you shall eat dust all the days of your life'" (Genesis 3:14, NKJV). Did you catch it? Satan was banned to eating *dust* all the days of his life. Adam, the first flesh created, *was made from dust.* If Satan is banned to eating only dust, then, spiritually speaking, *is it possible* that when we act on our fleshly desires by choosing to sin we are really feeding the enemy and making him stronger?

Satan, the king of counterfeit, is trying to shift the enmity (hostility, hate, antagonism, animosity, ill will) God placed between himself and us, to enmity between us and God and also men and women. As long as we have breath we have the awesome privilege of working *for* and *with* one another to reflect the Father to every heart on the planet. God wired our hearts with a need to know Him as Savior, but we also need one another to be a complete representation of the Father. **We were designed to work beautifully together to reflect the royal personhood of the triune.**

THE TWO SIDES OF GOD

Men often say, "We're simple. We're not complicated or hard to understand." Men also often ask, "Why do women have to be so complicated, overly emotional, and unpredictable? Why do they need so many shoes and purses? Why do they talk so much, and why do they have to make everything about feelings?"

Being a female, I would agree, women are more complex than men are; but evidently, He made us that way on purpose. Remember women are fluid and are built to pour over people, places, and things in their environments. They have more ability to change, adapt, and emotionally feel their way around obstacles. Men are solid, strong, and *physically* resilient. Women are, by design, more transparent and delicate and reflect many colors, while men are more black and white. **Yet, even with all of our differences, both men and women were made in the likeness**

of God. When we stand unified as partners, *men and women reflect the two distinct male and female sides of* God. Sometimes I think we forget what an *awesome privilege* that really is!

The more we study and ponder God's Word and seek and experience His presence, the more we realize His multifaceted character and the depth of His true personhood. **To begin to understand that God is a person, with power, wisdom, and emotions is fascinating.** When we open up our minds to His true identity, the more we realize how many parts He has to *His being.* Knowing Him causes us to know how much bigger, greater, and wiser He is than we are in every way.

God is indescribable, but He can be revealed in the male and female relationships of love and commitment. We get to be a partial reflection of Him when we accept Him, believe Him, and yield to His personhood inside of us. His thoughts and characteristics are deeper than the deepest ocean. I like to think of His character as an indescribable, gigantic diamond of the highest cut, color, and clarity imaginable. As we hold His character in the light and turn it, with every millimeter of the rotation, the light shines through, bounces off another facet, and reflects still another color or image of who He really is! We can never know everything there is to know about Him, but this is what makes this journey with Him so exhilarating. The more hungry and open we are to Him, the more hints of His awesomeness and character we experience in preparation for what we will someday know and understand when we see Him in His glorious majesty in heaven.

Men and women are different but both reflect equally powerful and important parts of God and His character. Women are the feminine, nurturing, gentle side of God and fit safely under the provision and protection of the masculine, male warrior side of God.

Could it be this seemingly more complex, colorful, and, dare I say, complicated reflection of God might be some of what he had on His mind when He chose to fashion Eve as the first female? **Women are compelled to bring color and beauty into the world.** Being the feminine side of God, *women gravitate to creating something beautiful or bringing appreciation or expression to it.* We must recognize Satan is not omnipresent and can't read our minds or our futures, but he and his demons study our behavior. I wonder if Satan noticed in the garden that Eve had an intense desire to gravitate toward beauty and notice things around her that Adam might not have. Women of all ages are wired to do this. They collect pieces (sometimes the broken pieces of their lives or someone else's) and try to create something beautiful from them. Much like a mosaic artist tries to make a beautiful picture, plate, or piece of furniture out of broken pieces of china or glass, a woman sees the potential in people and tries to cultivate that into something beautiful. She often tries to glue the broken pieces into something solid and then pours heart and soul over it to bring stability and connection. Women are compelled and designed to do this; however, she needs balance because often the very things God put inside her as a gift, if not sifted constantly through the guidance and direction of the Holy Spirit, can destroy her. (This is also true for men.)

Guys, I will even venture to say that often women don't fully understand the depths and complexities of themselves either. This is why a woman needs the strength of a man to balance her. **There are times when women don't fully understand what's going on in their bodies physically. Hormonal changes beyond her control cause her to have emotions that are sometimes embarrassing and, in some cases, scary.** Take for instance, her monthly cycle, pregnancy, and menopause. Often her body is evolving and the physiology is causing emotional and physical changes she doesn't always understand and finds it difficult to manage. There are times when she may not have a warning that changes are coming or how to deal with them. The fluidity of her emotions often caused by physical changes beyond her control is something she is forced to adapt and yield to. Her body has a cycle just like the planets. Just as men are positioned and designed to become nurturing shepherds, strong warriors, successful hunters, and good kings, women are positioned and designed to be moving, changing, vibrant, colorful, powerful, tender, and delicate royalty.

Men by nature are warriors and kings; therefore, they automatically *conceal* instead of choosing to *reveal*. They tend to have a hard time letting their guard down and being vulnerable with the women who care about them. For most men, this is not natural or easy. He must learn how to reveal his feelings. This gives the women in his life (wives, daughters, mothers, sisters, friends) the emotional intimacy, security, and nurturing they need, which only comes when he learns to be emotionally and verbally vulnerable. Tears are nothing to be ashamed of when sharing authentic feelings. A man's humility and authenticity will usually open a female heart to him. This move often results in her trusting him and creates a strong sense of partnership. The Lord knew it would be hard for men, but he may have planned to use this as a transformation tool, making them more like Jesus. **God doesn't promise to make us *comfortable*. He allows things in our lives to make us *holy*. He wants us to learn to be givers, not takers, so He created opportunities for us to sacrifice, serve others, and be purified through the process.**

THE MASCULINE AND FEMININE PARTS OF GOD

If the male is the masculine (provider, protector, and leader) part of God the Father, then the female is the feminine (collector, connector, and supporter) side of Him. When the masculine and feminine are confident and in position, unity abounds and God's powerful, multifaceted character is reflected to a lost and dying world.

Guys, I believe with all my heart most of you really want to get this right. You want to be whole, content, loved, and successful as providers, friends, leaders, sons, husbands, and fathers. You don't want to fail; God wired you to win for you *and* for her. Take heart, if you are a follower of Christ and have the Holy Spirit living in you, you have the awesome ability to not only be transformed and sanctified but to reflect His glory.

Girls, I believe with all my heart most of you really want to get this right. You want to be whole, content, loved, and successful connectors, nurturers, life givers, daughters, wives, and moms. Take heart, if you are a follower of Jesus and have the Holy Spirit living in you, you not only get to reflect the emotional, sensitive, creative part of Father God but you, too, get to reflect His glory.

Both parts can work perfectly together when they choose to yield to the Holy Spirit and lay down the need to completely understand, be in control, always win, or be right. It is a moment-by-moment decision to stop and ask:

"God, what do You want to say to me about myself?"

"God what do You want to change in me?"

"God what do You want to say to me about You?"

PAUSE, PONDER, PRAY, AND OBEY

MEN AND WOMEN:

1. Make a list of the women and men who play an important role in your life.

2. After you have written down the names, write out the positive attributes you see in them.

3. Write down how you think they see themselves? Do you think they believe the truth or lies about themselves? If so, what might those lies be?

4. Do you think they are aware of their inner beauty? Why or why not?

5. How do you think God sees them?

6. What can you do to help them see their worth and value to God and step up and into the position God created for them?

Pray now and ask the Lord to show you how He sees them and what your part is in their lives. Ask Him to show you how to help them take their rightful place within God's perspective.

What is the Holy Spirit saying to you? Take some time to find three scripture verses that encourage you or confirm what you are hearing.

_____

_____

_____

_____

_____

_____

_____

_____

_____

_____

_____

_____

_____

_____

_____

_____

_____

_____

_____

_____

_____

_____

_____

_____

_____

_____

_____

_____

_____

_____

_____

_____

_____

_____

_____

_____

_____

_____

_____

*And the glory which You gave Me I have given them,
that they may be one just as We are one: I in them, and
You in Me; that they may be made perfect in one, and
that the world may know that You have sent Me, and
have loved them as You have loved me.*
John 17:22–23 (NKJV)

Chapter 5

KEYS OF TRUTH ABOUT MEN

My hope is this section of the book will not only help men get a better understanding of who they are, but also help women see men through new lenses. As I began to apply these truths to my life and our marriage, Don began to open up to me. Something began shifting in our relationship. When we had conversations, he became *more engaged* and *less guarded* and *defensive*. One day he came to me with a trusting, playful smile on his face and said, "I'm not sure what you're doing, but I feel like a guinea pig with benefits ... *and I like it!*" We laughed, but the message was loud and clear—he *liked* the benefits, and I did too! We had become partners rather than adversaries, and we *both* loved it!

Men, if you are having trouble getting women to see you as their leader, get alone with God and ask Him to show you how women see you and how you see women. Remember to pause, ponder, pray, and obey what the Lord reveals to you about them and about yourself. Do you believe God will give you the discernment and courage to know when and how to battle and war for your family and the women in your life? Will you have the courage to step up and into your masculinity to protect and nurture the females in your world? Are you ready and willing to courageously take your position so they can confidently take theirs?

Ladies, if you will open your hearts, you will see how truly remarkable men are, what a gift they are to you, and that you were not designed to live without them. Understanding these simple truths has changed the relationships with the men in my life and created an atmosphere of trust, honor, and respect between us.

WARNING! Ladies, these keys of truth may seem simple, but they are very powerful to opening up a man's heart, so it's important to handle the men in your lives with care. God wired men to be *rational* and *discerning*, and they tend to focus more on *facts than feelings*. As hunters, warriors, and kings, men need this skill set in their arsenal. They are able to strategically win wars, hunt large animals, run companies, drive large machinery, and build almost anything. Because of their warrior minds, they can access facts and respond accordingly most of the time without letting emotions or feelings get in the way. They respect honor and are born to give it and expect it in return. Therefore, when women try to manipulate them, they recognize it (even if subconsciously), and it almost always backfires. So it's important to be careful *not* to ever use any of these keys to manipulate men. It will do great damage to a man's heart *and* to your relationship with

> him. Take time to pray before you begin using a key of truth, and ask the Lord for pure motives when you do so. Partnering with God and having pure motives when speaking a truth brings benefits to both you and the men in your life.

Ladies, are you ready to learn some simple yet profound truths about the males in your life? Men, are you ready to learn more about yourselves? Let's get started!

KEYS OF TRUTH ABOUT MEN

> • • •
>
> As you begin identifying and understanding these keys of truth, you'll become more aware of and sensitive to them. I encourage you to notice (and take notes on) how these keys are proving true in your life and in the lives of the men around you. I'm sure you'll agree it's very fascinating once you have eyes to see.

1. **Men need partnership, and they love being part of a team.**

   Men not only need to be on a team with men, they also have a need to partner with women at every age and stage of their lives. **They want and need authentic, trustworthy partners who enjoy being a part of their team.** This partnership brings love, gratitude, respect, and security for *both* genders.

   Conversely, competition between males and females fuels adversarial relationships and breaks partnerships because they are no longer on the *same* team. Overly competitive women often emasculate men, and when a man feels emasculated, his masculinity is drained and, over time, he will cease to provide and protect.

It's important for women to learn to allow men to play *for* them. This is particularly fun when playing games. I love playing cornhole (or beanbag toss) with my family, especially when I can partner with Don, my son Jonathan, or my son-in-law Jon. When we are on the same team, we immediately bond, because they love to feel they are winning *for* me (and they usually are!).

Men, your score is not as important as her heart. There are times men bring the winning mentality into the emotional part of a relationship, which can cause resentment and damage to a female's heart. There are times when, to a man, winning or being right is everything. I promise you, because of your strength and size, this position will destroy the relationships with the women in your life. **God asks us to pause (take a moment and stop reacting), ponder (think about what God's Word says is really true), pray (ask the Lord what He has to say about it), and then obey (whatever He says, even if it is hard and we don't fully understand).** Be patient with yourself and do the next right thing as He directs.

As we lay down our agendas and partner with and for each other, the more we will see God move in our hearts and sanctify us. We will also learn how trustworthy He is when we team up with the Creator of the Universe. The truth is, He desires for men and women to be fully reconciled to one another and one in Christ (Galatians 3:28). When that happens, the results are always miraculous.

2. Men are attracted to women who are feminine and confident.

Men enjoy women who embrace their femininity, yet are confident. Men desire friendship and partnership with women. A poised partner and confident teammate makes a man look and feel successful. Healthy men don't like needy women or women who act like "silly girls." He is looking for a Queen to partner with him. They like women who know who they are. On the other hand, if a woman won't let a man do things for her, or she is domineering, demanding, bossy, condescending, or overly assertive toward him, he will disengage and, over time, emotionally disconnect from her altogether. Nothing makes a man feel more attractive, masculine, and successful than a content, confident woman who allows him to care for her.

A confident woman is fun, but she is also extremely sure about who she is and knows her position. She recognizes she needs a man's covering and knows her identity as an individual *and* as a partner. **A feminine and radiant woman is a reflection of the man who covers her.**

Most women know they are *supposed* to submit to their husbands and men who have godly authority in their lives, but we rarely hear—even in the church—exactly *how* to submit the way God intended. God created us and put an order in place so we can all thrive in our positions with one another and live as helpers and partners. **When guys think women don't want or need their provision or protection, they tend to behave in a highly competitive way. When they feel emasculated, they feel a need to prove their masculinity.** When a female acts masculine, it doesn't bring out the best in a man. This has nothing to do with sexuality. Women need to remember one of the primary things men tend to fear is not being enough, or *appearing* to be not enough, for the women in his life.

3. Men like to be around women who are fun and have a sense of humor.

Many times a man is attracted to a woman because of how much fun they have together. Men thrive in fun environments, not just with other men, but with women too. Our culture says men like to laugh *at* women, but the truth is they love to laugh *with* women. A guy likes a girl who can take a joke and knows how to laugh with him (and sometimes at herself). Women with a sense of humor make the adventure more valuable and exciting. They create joy instead of heaviness.

4. Men notice a woman's smile.

A genuine smile from a woman can light up a man's world. Contrary to popular belief, men are interested in more than just sexual, seductive smiles from women. (Movies and TV shows have convinced us men only want women sexually, but this is not true of most men.) The kind of smile that attracts a good, respectable man is the kind that says, "I am emotionally healthy and balanced. I know who I am and enjoy life." If a woman smiles in a man's presence, he thinks he is doing a good job and has her approval, and he will more than likely continue to try to make her happy.

5. Men are wired to lead, not dominate.

God wants men to lead and shepherd like Jesus, because they are physically stronger. However, men must be careful to lead *with* His character and *in* His order. In every organization, including families, there must be a leader, not a dominator. A leader guides and shows the way, while a dominator seeks to take control. **A man who leads by domination will eventually create resentment and may cause a woman to shut down completely.** Jesus modeled leadership for men by leading with a perfect balance of humility, authority, tenderness, and strength. This type of leadership breeds trust and causes those under a man's care to rest under his covering.

6. Men need words of gratitude and verbal appreciation in public and in private.

Verbally showing honor and respect to a man with sincerity— both privately and publicly—causes the strengths of his character to grow and develop. When women choose to be vulnerable and voice things they like and respect about the men in their lives, it puts wind in their sails and liquid gold in their cups. **Two of the most powerful words to a man are "thank you."** When women target specific behaviors in men by expressing gratitude through words, attitudes, and actions, oftentimes those behaviors multiply. A man loves to know when he's doing something right because he measures his success by a woman's contentment. Men *want* to provide for and protect women who express appreciation for what they provide.

— • • • —

I never realized how important my words of gratitude and encouragement were to Don until I began to step outside of my comfort zone and become vulnerable by encouraging him with words of appreciation. Once I did that, he began to trust me more and more. It didn't happen quickly. It took a while for him to trust me, because it was so foreign to him. I had covered and self-protected for so long that instead of trusting me right away, he wondered what I was up to.

We all need encouragement and whether women believe it or not, men need it as much as women do. For example, we might say to a co-worker or employee, "You're doing a great job!" "Thank you for being considerate of other's opinions." "Thank you for looking for ways to help and support the team." "People notice your integrity and character."

When standing with others, a wife, girlfriend, or friend might say, "He is so wise." "He does so much for us, and I appreciate so many things about him." "He is very good at what he does. Many people respect him in his field." "He is a great dad!" "He is a great husband." "He is a great man."

Women, ask God to show you the strengths in the men around you and to give you the courage to voice it.

7. **Men like women who respectfully ask for what they need or desire.**

Men don't like to *guess* what women need or desire. In fact, it feels cruel to men when women don't tell them what they want because it makes it hard for men to *provide* it for them. It feels like a game. It's frustrating to play the guessing game because men and women think so differently. Men feel defeated even before it starts because they know they rarely guess correctly. **Men don't like guessing, because they don't like to engage in something they don't think they can successfully accomplish.** When women respectfully ask men for what they need or desire, it sets them up to win. When a woman asks kindly, without an entitled attitude, she makes it easier for a man to give her what she needs as a *gift* and *not as a requirement.*

There are women who falsely believe if they're truly godly, they will sacrifice themselves by being "selfless," not needing or asking men for anything. But to men, they're not selfless, they're *frustrating.* I personally believe this lie has greatly *affected* and *infected* the body of Christ. Men cannot read women's minds and the silence creates great frustration for them. I've heard men say repeatedly, "If she will just tell me what she wants, I will try to provide it for her. I can't read her mind!" Women need to learn to see men as the strong providers they were made to be and help them succeed by respectfully communicating their needs and desires.

• • •

For years, I believed I was supposed to be silent and not ask Don for anything. Believing this lie created a lot of disappointment for both of us, which over time led to anger and bitterness in my heart toward Don because he didn't read my mind and provide what I wanted. I thought I was supposed to be quiet and pray and God would do the rest, but that false belief became very destructive to our relationship. In essence, I was expecting Don to know my expectations, which was so unfair to him.

• • •

Like many women I have known through the years, I did not fully understand what God meant by submission, so I would try to *will* myself to be submissive and selfless. When Don did not read my mind, I felt hurt and lonely, which caused me to grow resentful. What I thought was submission turned into complacency and self-protection. Soon I was in full self-protection mode, which led to an attitude of self-righteousness and anger that often surfaced by me emasculating Don.

It wasn't until I understood this key and began expressing my desires to Don that I realized how much he really wanted to provide *for* me. I just needed to have the courage to be vulnerable enough to tell him what I needed or what would thrill my heart. Once I did, it brought healing and freedom to our marriage. I am so thankful God forgives and restores relationships. He loves to help us to become better people and retrain us when we've gone off course.

8. Men need transition time.

Since men are single-focused, they need time to transition from one thing to another. For instance, when a man is just getting to work or just getting home, he needs transition time. It can take from 15 to 30 minutes, depending on how long he has been in the other place emotionally or physically. For example, when a man goes from a full day at the office to coming home to a wife (and kids), he needs time to transition. It's respectful to him when a woman realizes this and responds accordingly.

Men have a pattern and a way of transitioning and, more times than not, it will be the same way, in the same order, and take the same amount of time every day. For instance, when a man comes home after a long day at work, he may greet his wife and family, but he is not completely home yet. He may stop at the mailbox, sort the mail, go to the restroom, wash his face, change his clothes, and then come in and engage with the family. When we study the patterns of the men in our lives, we will see that the transition has become a ritual and is done the same way every day, so it is relatively easy to read. **It's respectful when a woman learns to greet him but doesn't immediately ask questions and begin trying to tell him about her day, because he may not be home yet emotionally. Once he's made the transition to being home, that's when he's able to fully connect and engage.**

Women who work outside the home full-time often adapt to the "male model" in the area of transition time. Women need the same consideration and transition time as a man. If you're married and you both work full-time, study each other and find a way to transition that works for both of you. (We will cover this more in the next chapter, "Keys of Truth About Women.")

● ● ●

I wish I had known this key years ago! It would have helped Don and me so much, especially when our kids were young. I would have been so much more considerate toward him and shown him more respect in this area. Being a stay-at-home mom often meant I was starving for adult conversation, so when Don came home, I would immediately bombard him with all the things I had connected with or collected throughout the day. He, on the other hand, would walk in the door after a long day at work with his guard up. Because he talked on the phone all day long, the last thing he wanted to do is walk in and start answering a bunch of questions. He just wanted to be quiet. So, the Lord led me to start allowing Don to have transition time. Once I learned to wait, Don no longer feared talking to me, and I no longer feared approaching him. He knew I was safe, and I knew he would be ready to connect with me after he had time to transition. I had not understood how important timing and transition were to him. I realized that to pour out the contents of my heart immediately after he got home caused him to feel overloaded, especially if he had not transitioned yet. It was difficult for him to shift quickly, and his immediate reaction was to tell me how to fix a problem I didn't know I had. Allowing him to have transition time kept my feelings from getting hurt whenever he seemed to be disinterested and detached.

9. **Men say what they mean and mean what they say.**

Men process differently than women and are usually more apt to trust facts than feelings, so when they're processing or taking a while to think, it's because they're accessing facts and information. Most of the time, it takes men a while to "find their feelings" and communicate them. Some men are undoubtedly more closed than others because of their backgrounds or upbringings, but men in general are deep and need time to process what they're feeling and find the courage to bring it into the light. In other words, when men are asked something that requires a feeling, they usually need time to express it.

Women want men to find their feelings and when they don't or can't, or it takes too long, some women feel a need to tell them *what* they should be feeling or *how* they should be feeling. (I used to be a master at this. I honestly thought I was helping the men in my life, but in reality, I was handicapping them.) If men want help, they will ask for it. **Most of the time, they don't need women to help them communicate, they just need time to *focus*.**

Ladies, there is nothing wrong with asking questions, but men, being single-focused, can get distracted easily and forget what they were thinking about or hunting for. Men don't like to be told how they feel, and they don't like to be interrupted. Women beg men to express their emotions because that's how women are wired but remember, men are *not* wired like women. Women desperately need to connect with their emotions, but the error is when they assume men have the same motivation.

Rather than reveal their emotions verbally, men tend to conceal them. (God may have included that for their warrior strategy.) However, when men do show emotions, they do it in a very different way than women. Men may not put words to their emotions quickly, but they do have ways of showing how they're feeling and often use nonverbal communication to express it. Sometimes it's through grunts and sounds, other times they express emotions through the upper portion of their bodies. When men feel happy, sad, angry, or excited, they usually show it in their chest, arms, and hands. They use different kinds of handshakes, strong pats, and gestures to communicate how they feel. For example, when a group of men are watching or playing sports, they often use high fives when they are really happy or satisfied and need to express it. Men may hug, but they usually include a strong slap on the back at the end of it as a way to release the energy and emotion they're feeling. They jump up and do chest bumps, or they reach for the helmet of their teammate to give them a shove.

10. **Men need women to bring emotional and physical color into their black-and-white worlds.**

Men can be very black and white in their thinking and the way they view life. Because they focus on facts, they don't look at the emotion connected to the words. Men are built for battle and can strategize and make decisions without getting caught up in the emotions of life. Yet they innately seem to know they need women, because they bring the emotional and physical color into their black-and-white worlds. Men see women as fascinating and mysterious, with a spontaneity that brings rhythm, movement, and texture into their lives. **Deep inside, men know women bring stability and keep their often wild sense of adventure grounded and balanced.** The changes bring transformation and are even part of the sanctification process because they are so different from one another.

It is wise for men to embrace the color, fragrance, and rhythm females bring into the atmosphere. When Jonathan moved back to Texas and built a new home as a bachelor, it was most definitely manly! Missing LA, he proudly hung one of his surfboards above the kitchen cabinets. Jonathan is extremely creative and has the ability to decorate, but his bachelor pad definitely lacked a feminine touch. When he brought his new bride, Laura, home, she embraced his love of surfing, but now there's also floral soap, soft towels, and tissue boxes in every bathroom, along with soft pillows tucked into the corners of the couch and scented candles filling the whole house with a sweet aroma. It's no longer a bachelor pad; it's now a warm and inviting home.

11. Men appreciate communication "bullet points."

Men tend to focus on the bottom line, and sometimes women have a tendency to go into a lot of detail when talking. This can cause men to tune them out or ignore them altogether. A man feels tortured when a woman goes on and on without a point. It's easier for them to stay focused when women talk in "bullet points." A woman who learns to think from a man's perspective will more likely be heard and get what she needs from him. When a woman is clear and to the point about what she needs or desires from a man, it makes it easier for him to *hunt successfully* and *provide* it for her.

Ladies, I have heard from men it's easier for them to listen more attentively *and* for longer if you begin your conversation with how many points you have. For example, you might say, "I have three things to talk to you about ...."

This is good for women in the workplace to remember as they communicate with their male co-workers, supervisors, and employees. It's important to be concise and clear in meetings, emails, and conversations with men. **Men don't need or want all the details—they just want the bullet points.**

It's also important to remember men *need* to find the point. It's helpful, before you begin a conversation, to ask yourself, "What is my point?" If there is no point, warn him all you need him to do is listen. Ask him if he would be willing to *hold the handle of your pitcher as you pour out* what you collected throughout the day. It is a huge gift to a man when a woman chooses to rephrase and speak in a way that allows him to know what she needs or that she just wants to share. Think before you begin! Being considerate to him and the way *he* thinks will help him hear what you want to say.

12. Men need and understand hero language.

Males of all ages and cultures understand and appreciate "hero language." Hero language speaks to a man's masculinity and makes him feel wise and strong. When a woman speaks hero language to a man, it suggests he is capable of covering her and providing what she needs. For example, a woman might say to a man, "I believe you'll make the right decision," "You know what to do," " I trust you," "Thank you for providing for me," "I know you'll figure this out," etc. It's important for women to use hero language because it speaks life into men. It says she believes he has what it takes, and God is going to give him the discernment to do the right thing. Hero language builds confidence and leadership in a man's heart toward a woman. It's important to remember this isn't true just for marriage, but for women in the workplace, especially those who supervise men.

Men need women to tell or remind them how strong they are. Men want to provide, and women need to *let them use their masculinity and show their strength*. Interestingly, there are many times a woman will struggle to do something herself instead of asking (or allowing) a man to do it for her.

EXAMPLES OF HERO LANGUAGE

- Can you help me?

- You're doing a great job!

- I really appreciate you.

- I need _____, would you mind helping me?

- You saved me by doing this for me!

- Wow, I really needed you!

- Thank you so much for _____ .

- I appreciate it when you _____ .

- You make me happy when you _____ .

- Thank you for going to work today.

- You make the right decisions.

- You will know what to do.

- I don't fear, because I know you have it.

- Thank you for leading me. When you lead, you make me feel safe.

- When you do that, I feel so valued and validated.

- Thank you for covering me and protecting me emotionally and physically. I could not be who I am without you.

- How can we work together as a team? I want to do this *with* you.

- I would choose you as my teammate/captain all over again.

- Thank you for traveling, I know you hate to be away and I miss you when you are gone, but I appreciate what you do for us every day.

I'm sure you get the idea. It is not a specific or exact phrase but an attitude of humility and gratitude that allows men to show their strength (emotionally, physically, and spiritually) to and for women.

13. Men appreciate women who know how to wait for responses without interrupting.

One of the best parts about men is they usually don't speak until they know what they want to say. So give them time to speak. **It's important to remember they are like telescopes— if they're interrupted, they lose their focus.** It's helpful when women give men the time they need to respond. They are not being difficult; they are being thorough.

Ladies, if you struggle with interrupting, a good way to practice this key is to learn to pause, ponder, and pray. Lean forward and put your hand over your mouth after you ask a question so you can wait effectively and not interrupt and distract him.

Men appreciate it when women wait for the correct timing and invite them to engage. For example, if a man is watching a football game, a woman should wait until the commercial to talk to him. Being respectful by waiting helps him respond in a more positive way. That way his focus isn't divided and he is fully engaged with her. Focusing on him, waiting to let him shift, not engaging in anything else while trying to get his attention is beneficial. Because men are like hunters, when women interrupt and don't give him time to come out of the "brush," think, and focus, he may forget what he was asked in the first place. This causes him to become frustrated because he has to refocus and start over. It helps a man to focus on what a woman is saying when she makes eye contact with him and has a pleasant and respectful attitude. This allows him to catch up with where her mind already is. Men feel emasculated and may lash out in anger when women talk for them (and over them) by adding words.

● ● ●

Men respond well to respectful communication. Here's a breakdown of how you can use these keys to better communicate with the men in your life.

- **Before communicating with a man, be aware he is looking for an opportunity to partner with you.**

  Men like to be partners, not adversaries, so speak words that communicate that you believe in him and your ability to work together to a good and productive end. Begin by saying things like, "I am confident we can work together on this and find a solution." "I *am on your side.*" "I know we can do this." or "What is my part? Is there anything I can do to help you?"

- **Ask for time to talk.**

  This shows respect for his time and gives him transition time to refocus on you. For example, I might say to Don, "I realize you may be busy now, but when you get a moment, I would love a few minutes to share something new with you." This says to him, that I am not going to chew him out for forgetting something and it won't take long.

- **If you're not upset, always include "I am not upset with you."**

  Men are more sensitive than women think. Most men dread hearing a woman say, "We need to talk," because they think they're in trouble. When it comes to important topics, whether it's about the kids, work, or your relationship, a man appreciates when a woman requests a time for him to talk and lets him pick the time, which allows him to be more focused. In other words, she could say, "Is there a time I can have a few minutes to talk to you? It can be later. What time works best for you?" Let him know if it will only take a few minutes, and let him know that he's not in trouble or that you're not upset.

- **Always express your appreciation.**

  Be sure to thank him for what He has already done or provided for you and/or the family. Be courageous, and tell him what you sincerely like and appreciate about *him*.

- **Look for opportunities to use hero language.**

- **When you have a need (or desire) he is capable of fulfilling, ask for it with as few words as possible, which makes a man feel relieved and happy.**

You can tell a man *what* to do or you can tell him *how* to do it, but don't do both. Telling him both can feel emasculating and disrespectful to him.

- **If your request requires time to accomplish, ask him to let you know the progress as he works so you will know he has begun and not forgotten.** Ask him if he thinks it would be fair to inquire if you don't see any progress.

When you see signs he is providing any part of what you asked him for, express verbal or written appreciation for his efforts and tell him the difference it is making for you and how validated and/or safe it makes you feel.

14. Men don't like to be mothered.

Often in our culture, spouses treat children like spouses and spouses like children. While men like to be cared for and sometimes even nurtured, they don't like to be treated like a child or to feel patronized. Mothering strips a man of his masculinity and cuts him to the core. This sometimes causes a man to shut down emotionally, and he will eventually stop trying to provide and protect. Many times women see the potential in the men in their lives and want to encourage them; however, this encouragement can be perceived by men as mothering and causes them to become defensive.

> Ladies, ask your husbands, boyfriends, or co-workers to signal you if you are mothering them. If it has become a habit or you saw it in your family growing up, ask him to give you a subtle signal when you are doing it.

15. Men distance themselves from women when they feel criticized.

Men are highly sensitive to criticism. Some women believe criticism creates a desire within a man to change, because that's how most women are wired. Yet with men, it often causes the opposite response. When men feel criticized, they disconnect because it feels emasculating. Encouragement and praise bring about more change in most men than criticism.

● ● ●

One of my girlfriends oversees a team that handles corporate communication. One of the male team members had written something that contained incorrect information, and when she noticed it, she called to let him know. As she was explaining what was wrong and what needed to be changed, he snapped at her and hung up the phone before she could even say goodbye. Because she had been to a Keys of Truth Conference and learned this key, she realized she may have relayed the information in a way that made him feel criticized and inadequate, which caused him to feel emasculated and shut down completely. The next day she took time to meet with him and talk about what happened. Sure enough, he confirmed she had made him feel stupid by the way she had communicated the mistake to him. Her awareness of the keys of truth helped her remedy the problem *and* find a more beneficial way to communicate in the future. Now she courageously watches and recognizes how to communicate more effectively with men and women.

16. Men need outlets and hobbies.

Some men enjoy golf. Some enjoy reading books or watching movies. For some it's fishing, hunting, going to the beach, or being out in creation at the lake or in the country. For most men, these outlets and hobbies fulfill their need for competition and adventure. There are times men may invite women to be a part of an outing, but sometimes they just want time with guys or time alone. If a man does invite a female to join him, what he is most interested in is her presence. **During these adventures, most men don't want conversation; they simply desire "shoulder to shoulder" companionship with her.** It seems strange to women, but men feel very connected and content when sitting silently shoulder to shoulder with people who are important to them. During these times, men just want to relax and not have to provide for or protect anyone.

Warning! Men, as with all of life, the balance of outings and hobbies is important. When your outlet becomes the only thing you're passionate about or all you want to do, it feels like rejection to the women in your life, which may eventually turn into fear, pain, and resentment.

• • •

A friend's husband invited her to go deer hunting with him. She decided she would "gift" her husband with her presence. Being a "girly girl," she knew it would be a big sacrifice, but she was thrilled he invited her into his space and was anxious to prove her love for her man by going with him.

When the day came, they rose early, loaded into his pick-up truck, and traveled out into the woods to get positioned in the deer blind. They sat silently for hours, which seemed like weeks to her. Periodically, she would glance over at her husband's face. He was obviously content sitting there in total silence—he had his woman and was ready to prove his hunting skill to her. He felt like he was in heaven! As minutes turned into hours, *he* stayed content and happy, while *she* grew cold, stiff, uncomfortable, and more miserable by the moment. All she kept thinking was, *If we could just talk, our time together would be so much more fun and fulfilling!*

On their way home after an entire day of hunting, he reached over the front seat of the truck and grabbed her hand and said, "Thank you so much for coming with me! That was one of the best days I've had with you in a *long* time!"

Later, my sweet friend confessed she doubted she would ever go hunting again. She loved spending time with him, but the silence was excruciating to her! I'm sure most women can relate. To a woman silence can be torture, but to a man it can be exhilarating.

(I wonder if this was a female sanctification test given by the Lord? If so, I think she passed!)

17. Men work for success.

Men focus on *doing* not *trying*. Because they are warriors and hunters, they must see the potential to succeed. For example, if a hunter is hunting for food, he needs to make sure his shot hits the target; otherwise, he might become the food. When a man goes into battle, he has to believe he will be the victor or he already feels defeated. **When men don't see a strong possibility for success, they usually won't try.** This is also true for men in relationships. God wired men to war and win as individuals and as teammates. He needs to feel he will attain success in her eyes or he will not continue trying. A female's attitude and gratitude toward a man will make or break his desire to provide for and protect her.

18. Men need women who will let them learn.

Men need opportunities to learn how to do new things. When women criticize men, it makes them feel stupid and incapable. He needs to prove his masculinity by figuring it out himself. In other words, if she asks him to diaper the baby, then stands over him and tells him how he should do it or how he is doing it wrong, he won't ever learn and he'll cease to try. The same is true when washing dishes, loading the dishwasher, folding clothes, driving the car, planning dates, or scheduling vacations. Men also need women to let them learn in the workplace when it comes to planning a presentation or preparing for a meeting. Whatever it is, men won't try unless they think they can figure it out *and* do it successfully. Women must give them space and grace along with the opportunity to learn.

● ● ●

This key proves to be inborn time and time again. I can remember the first time I saw this in Jonathan when he was two years old. I thought he was just being stubborn. We were out in the driveway, and he was trying to learn how to ride his new trike. He was pushing down on both pedals with equal force at the same time and, of course, going nowhere fast! He was getting furious and starting to cry. I bent down beside him and tried to help him by pressing just one foot and saying, "One foot at a time." He would get furious and say, "Mom, I do it myself!" I still remember wondering why something so insignificant was making him so angry at *me*. Don walked out of the garage and told me Jonathan needed to figure it out on his own, which he eventually did. But the mom in me found it frustrating and hard to watch.

About six years later, we were at the lake, and Don and I were in a boat anchored to a buoy in a cove. Jonathan and Holly were in a canoe, and the current and waves began to cause them to drift away from us. Jonathan was about eight years old and had not yet learned how to paddle using oars. Don stood and watched for a while and saw Jonathan was getting angrier by the minute as they repeatedly went around and around in circles, while Holly was just sitting there enjoying the view, probably singing a song to Jonathan about fish swimming in the lake. I wanted Don to jump in and swim over and help him! But Don (being a male) calmly yelled out one or two instructions to him and then said, "He'll figure it out, just give him time." Sure enough, he did! Don knew Jonathan *needed to* and *would* figure it out on his own. And you know what? He eventually did.

19. Men may assume an automatic attack mode when they feel disrespected.

When men are disrespected, it often makes them feel threatened, and the warrior in them comes out emotionally or verbally swinging. When a woman disrespects a man, it makes him feel like she thinks he doesn't know what he's doing and is stupid and incapable of protecting her and providing for her needs and/or the needs of the family. It's part of a man's DNA to be a provider and protector, so when that gets undermined, he can go into self-protection mode by distancing, disconnecting, and dishonoring her. When he feels disrespected, he'll begin to show frustration—he may get a look or an attitude that signals his displeasure. It's selfless and courageous to ask him if you have done or said something that made him feel emasculated.

● ● ●

Throughout our marriage, I would offer suggestions to Don with regard to things around the house, thinking I was helping him. He would immediately become frustrated and defensive. **I know now that he perceived my "help" as my lack of confidence in him and his abilities.** This was not at all my motive or intention, but my motive had nothing to do with what he was feeling. It was life changing for me when I began to understand more about this truth and see what triggered the "warrior mode" in Don.

20. Men live by an unwritten honor code.

Have you ever noticed that boys and men tend to live by an unwritten honor code? It may be unspoken but if you ask a man, it is very real. Men are hard-wired to honor one another. They don't talk bad about other men unless they have to (probably because one of them broke the silent honor code). Maybe the masculinity and the team gene in men bring an adherence to the honor code because of their need for survival, hunting, and battlefield situations. Even with the gender lines more blurred than ever before in our culture, the honor code still remains intact for most men.

PAUSE, PONDER, PRAY, AND OBEY

MEN:

1. How do you feel about the keys for men?

2. Do you agree with the keys of truth about men? Why or why not?

3. Are there any you can't relate to? If so, which ones?

4. What did you learn about yourself that you did not know?

5. When was the last time you felt emasculated? How did you respond?

6. How does it feel to be emasculated in front of other people?

   a. How do you respond?

   b. Do you ignore it and shove the feelings down or do you share how it made you feel with the person who emasculated you? Why or why not?

7. Say a prayer to the Lord asking for forgiveness for any men you may have emasculated.

8. Say a prayer and ask the Lord to help you forgive those who have emasculated you and may not have even known it.

9. Pray and ask the Lord to help you forgive those who may have taught you false beliefs about men, understanding they may not have known the truth.

10. Write down how you are going to apply what you have learned.

WOMEN:

1. Did you learn anything new about men from reading these keys of truth about men?

2. What did you learn about men that you did not know?

3. Where did your views and beliefs about men come from? Are most of your views about men accurate or inaccurate? Are your views healthy or unhealthy for you and those around you?

4. Are there any lies you have believed about men? If so, what are they?

5. Pray and ask the Lord to forgive you for the lies you have believed about men.

6. How do you think it feels to a man to be emasculated?

7. How do you think it feels to be emasculated in front of

other people?

8. Pray and ask the Lord to forgive you for times you have intentionally or unintentionally emasculated men.

9. Pray and ask the Lord if there are any men you need to ask for forgiveness.

10. Pray and ask the Lord to reveal the truth to you about men.

11. Pray and ask the Lord to help you forgive those who may have taught you incorrectly about men, understanding they may not have known the truth.

12. Write down how are you going to apply what you've learned?

MEN AND WOMEN:

For the next few days or weeks, observe the males around you:

- How do men respond when they feel emasculated and dishonored?

- How do they respond when they feel honored and respected?

- Listen to what they say, watch their faces and body language, and make notes.

There are three desires written deeply into a male heart:

1. A battle to fight,
2. An adventure to live, and
3. A beauty to rescue.

Adapted from *Wild at Heart* by John Eldredge[11]

What is the Holy Spirit saying to you? Take some time to find three scripture verses that encourage you or confirm what you are hearing.

_____

_____

_____

_____

_____

_____

_____

_____

_____

_____

_____

_____

_____

_____

_____

_____

_____

_____

_____

_____

_____

_____

_____

_____

_____

_____

_____

_____

_____

_____

_____

_____

_____

_____

_____

_____

_____

_____

Summing it all up, friends, I'd say you'll do best by filling your minds and meditating on things true, noble, reputable, authentic, compelling, gracious—the best, not the worst; the beautiful, not the ugly; things to praise, not things to curse. Put into practice what you learned from me [God's Word], what you heard and saw and realized. Do that, and God, who makes everything work together, will work you into his most excellent harmonies.
Philippians 4:8–9 (MSG)

Chapter 6

KEYS OF TRUTH ABOUT WOMEN

The following keys of truth about women will help men care for, provide for, empower, and protect the girls and women in their lives. These keys will also help women understand themselves, their daughters, and their friends better. It's quite extraordinary once we begin to see these as a whole.

Working with and teaching women for more than 20 years has allowed me to learn a lot about them. I believe each woman deeply desires to drop her sword, remove her dented battle gear, and be held by the man who is protecting her. (He may be her daddy, boyfriend, friend, brother, or husband.) Regardless of what women say or how they behave, many who appear domineering and rough on the outside are girls who just want to know they are worth the fight.

Because of our culture's confusion about male and female roles, many women, especially Christian woman, are wondering where the strong, courageous men have gone. While men are responsible for their own actions, I believe Western culture and women affected by it may have scared some men into dropping their swords, suggesting they need to be more passive and less masculine. Adding to the confusion is the nonverbal suggestion to young women that it's weak to even suggest, much less admit, they need a man in their lives.

As a female, I bought into that lie without even knowing it! Deep down women know they need men, but they feel it's dangerous to let down their guards and trust men to fight for them. I have known women who feel a sense of shame and panic when they even think about ceasing to fight for themselves. Don't get me wrong, as Christian women we do need to fight the enemy and wield the sword of the Spirit (which is God's Word), but to fight against the male gender is ignorant and plays into the enemy's hands! He is using it as a diversion tactic so we don't wield the power we have toward *him*.

Most of us know more than a few amazingly beautiful, talented, successful, single Christian women who are battle weary and yearn for partnership with a godly man. Some women believe that because they're single they must be strong and appear independent in order for men to desire them or to keep from being abused and used by them. Sadly, it's this mind-set causing many men to feel intimidated and inadequate because these women don't need them or want them. Because of the damage done over the past 50 years, women today need to know how to send men signals to let men know they want and need their masculinity, and it's up to the men to step up and give it.

Women need to know God wired men to be drawn to confident, smart, balanced women who want to partner with them.

Emotionally healthy men instinctively know in order to take their positions, they need a woman who can take hers. It builds courage in a man to be around a woman who allows him to fulfill his God-ordained position and successfully provide for and protect her.

Ladies, if you are having trouble getting men to see you as a valuable partner, get alone with God and ask Him to show you how men see you and how you see men. Remember to pause, ponder, pray, and obey what the Lord reveals to you. Embrace your feminine strengths and wisdom. Be brave, lay down your sword of emasculation, and take off your battle gear. It may be hard, because it is *counter-cultural*. Taking your biblical position in today's world takes practice and attention. The first hurdle is trusting God to help you do it His way. Do you believe God will give you the discernment to know when, how, and who to submit to and the courage to step up and begin? Will you believe the best about the men in your life? Will you believe God wired them to provide for and protect you? Will you believe real men want something to fight for? Will you believe this something just might be *you*?

WARNING! Men, just as I warned women in your section about not using these keys to manipulate, I want to warn you not to use these keys to bully the women in your life. It's easy for a man to insert his masculinity to get women to do what he wants. Take time to pray before you begin using a key of truth, and ask the Lord for pure motives. Partnering with God and having pure motives when speaking a truth brings benefits to both you and the women in your life.

Guys, on the following pages are some keys to help you understand the women in your life. Some of them will surprise you and some you may not fully understand, but if you will choose to observe the women in your world, you may find the keys are not only true but also helpful.

Ladies, I believe by reading this section, you will be relieved to find out you are not strange but quite normal. Women often think they are the only ones who behave or feel a certain way. On these pages, you will find out you are not alone. Read on ladies, and take heart!

KEYS OF TRUTH ABOUT WOMEN

> ● ● ●
>
> As you begin identifying and understanding these keys of truth about women, you'll become more aware and sensitive to them. I encourage you to take some time to observe others and make notes as you see how these keys are proven true in your life and in the lives of the women around you. I'm sure you'll agree it's very fascinating once you have eyes to see.

1. Women have a "female fear factor."

Because females are the physically more vulnerable of the two genders, God may have wired them with a natural heightened sensitivity to danger for their own safety. I understand this is not politically correct and, in many ways, counter-cultural. Women are emotionally very strong, but I have seen the "female fear factor" proven true time and time again.

● ● ●

When I share about this key in conferences, I start out by asking a question of the men and then the women. First, I ask men to raise their hands if they've feared for their personal safety in the past month. Rarely do any hands go up. Then I ask *women* to raise their hands if they've feared for their personal safety in the past month. The majority of the women, if not all, raise their hands. Then I ask if they've feared in the past week? Hands stay up. Yesterday? Hands are still up.

During this exercise, it becomes extremely obvious men and women are *very* different, if not opposite in the area of physical fear. Men are shocked when they see most, if not all, of the women in the room feel fear for their personal safety almost daily. (The last time they felt fear might have been in the car with their husbands driving to the conference.) **Men are surprised to hear *women are always on high alert* when walking through an airport, shopping mall, or parking lot alone. It does not usually occur to a man to be afraid in the same situation.**

As warriors and hunters, men are not wired to fear. In war movies, such as *The Patriot*, men courageously line up for battle and face their enemy—often dying in the process. You don't see a lot, if any, movies with women going into battle, especially not on the frontlines. Could it be that it's just not realistic because it's not God's design and order for women?

If a female perceives something is a threat—it may not truly be a threat, but she *perceives* it to be—she will give a signal that her senses are on high alert. She may make a strange facial expression or blurt out a noise. She may put her hands up to her face or mouth. Her eyes may widen or squint. Regardless, she *will* have a physical reaction until the threat leaves, she gets away from it, or she can connect with it in a positive way. She may not always say she is fearful, but her face, voice, and body language will usually let you know, if you pay attention. As she matures spiritually, she will learn to depend more on God, and the fragile parts of her may become more resilient as she walks with Him. If you want to know what a female is feeling, study her. God helped us out by the way He wired her to show her feelings, but we have to stop, focus on her, and take mental notes.

There are times when women react out of fear by saying things or acting in certain ways that make the people in their lives feel disrespected, which for men can feel emasculating. A woman's fear often surfaces when she is riding in a car (especially when she is not driving). Sometimes it surfaces when someone she cares about is doing something she perceives as dangerous such as hunting or driving a motorcycle. This fear regularly manifests itself through questions. Women may ask: "Are you sure you want to do that?" "What if it doesn't work?" "Do you know what you are doing?" "Are you sure this is safe for the kids?" Men, in particular, don't see this as women needing reassurance and comfort (which is most often the case), they see it as women thinking they're irresponsible, inadequate, and stupid.

It might be that God built this "female fear factor" into a woman's heart because of her size and position. He may allow women to feel fear to cause them to depend upon men to cover and provide for them—after all, protection is what men *need* to give. Most men don't understand how physically fragile women sometimes feel and the fear that comes with that. There is great power when a man learns *how* to offer his strength to make a woman feel safe.

● ● ●

1 Peter 3:7 talks about women as the weaker of the two genders: "Husbands in the same way be considerate as you live with your wives and treat them with respect as a weaker partner and as heirs with you as a greater gift of life so that nothing will hinder your prayers." Could this mean the vessel females live in may be more vulnerable physically? I'm not saying men are not vulnerable, because as humans they are, but because of women's muscle mass and bone density, women, married and single, are physically more vulnerable.

Christian women know they're not *supposed* to be afraid, but many of the women I know struggle with it for most of their lives. Most women battle fear at some point in their lives, and **when a woman does not feel important or covered by the men in her life, her fear will rapidly intensify.** Jesus said more than once in the Bible to "fear not," and as a woman begins to trust the Lord, her fear decreases dramatically. As she becomes more sanctified, she becomes less and less fearful. She may feel concern, but she chooses to trust the Lord and receive His peace.

When a woman partners with a man (or men) she trusts, her confidence grows, and her fear diminishes, because she doesn't have to prove anything to herself or to those she is partnering with. It's also easier for her to step into her position when the men around her represent the Savior well. By experientially knowing God, her confidence and grace will begin to outweigh her fear. Yet, because of the confusion in our culture, this process takes time. Through experience, men and women can learn how to take their positions while discovering and appreciating how extraordinarily God created both males and females.

Men, how do you respond when females show fear? Have you ever considered why she acts the way she acts or feels the way she feels?

Men, consider that a woman's reaction is *not* usually rooted in her mistrust of you or her believing that you are ignorant. Her fear is not a need to control you but more her need *for* you. She subconsciously (or consciously) knows she is physically more vulnerable and is not capable of protecting herself (or you) if she finds herself in a dangerous situation. When you participate in an activity or behavior she sees as risky, she may be wondering what life would be like if something happened to you. If you are gone, who will be at your post providing for and protecting her? She needs you, and she knows it.

If you did something to trigger her fear, don't ignore it or blame it on her. Ignoring a woman's fear (or pain) can cause her to slide deeper into an emotional pit. If you are not sure it was something you said or did, have the courage to ask her, "Did I hurt your feelings or do something to scare you?"

Eye contact, a compassionate smile, and/or non-sexual touch will comfort her, help her gain trust in you, and come back to you. Prove you are trustworthy by taking time to connect with her. Having the courage to address it can lessen the depth of damage later. Her fear is something she will battle most of her life, and you can help her to keep it in perspective or diminish it substantially.

●●●

It's exciting to discover God may have also given females a completely different set of keys of truth to help counter her fear and to compensate for her being the smaller, physically weaker of the genders. I can hardly wait to share them with you in this chapter.

2. Women have a radar (and it is never off unless she is asleep).

God wired most women with a very sensitive and efficient "radar system" because of her size and the physical vulnerability associated with it. This radar allows a woman to be very aware of her environment and serves as an alert system, not only for her but also for those she is responsible for and cares about. This is especially true for moms with children, yet it is also in full swing when they are in a work environment or out by themselves. When women are in a restaurant or large gathering places, their emotional radar is "beeping," and it's because they're always aware of who and what is nearby and around them.

A woman's radar allows her to think about many things at once and helps her to multitask effectively. It also makes it hard for her to focus on just *one* thing at a time. A woman can stir a pot of chili on the stove, talk on the phone to another mom about carpool, greet her husband, *and* think about a meeting at work the next day—*almost* all at the same time. A woman's radar also helps her keep track of where each family member is.

While this is a great strength, it can be exhausting and deplete her energy. It is difficult or almost impossible for a woman to turn her radar off (or even down) unless she is asleep, because it's involuntary. This is why so many women love to go to a funny or romantic movie or a quiet dinner in a dimly lit room alone with her man or her girlfriends. Some men think women desire an expensive romantic dinner and she expects him to deliver something emotionally deep and extravagant. But honestly, what most women prefer is a quiet place to allow her radar to slow so she can relax and *just be.*

It's difficult for most women to function well (or be creative) without ample rest, so they need ways to slow down their radar enough to allow them to go to sleep. Reading a book, listening to music, praying, watching TV, or engaging in simple quiet conversation before they go to sleep are great ways women can slow their radar down.

I can't just "turn off" at the end of a long, busy day. I love watching movies at the theater, because I can completely disconnect with ease. (Order me popcorn with a half Dr Pepper/half Diet Dr Pepper, and I'm a happy girl!) At home, I watch TV because reading makes me feel like I'm ignoring Don. I like to watch TV shows that engage me—not sports or silly comedies—they must have a storyline I can follow and enter into. It's one of the best ways for me to completely disconnect.

3. Women are highly adaptable.

One of the most valuable and beautiful things God wired into women is their ability to adapt. Women can become highly successful and extremely valuable because of their ability to acclimate. Yet there can be a downside to this. **A woman who feels a need to provide for and protect herself and her children has a tendency to adapt so much that she will drive her body into the ground.** Over time, these women may suffer from adrenal burnout and other stress-related diseases because their bodies were not built to carry that much *physical* and *emotional* stress at the same time. More importantly, her feminine needs are often ignored. Adaptability was wired into females for a purpose, but studies show that when it is excessive and out of balance it can lead to depression, exhaustion, and can eventually destroy her physically.[12]

God knew women needed adaptability because in some cases, more often than fathers, mothers might find themselves raising children alone. They may be military wives or have husbands who travel or they may have gone through a divorce or have been widowed. When a father is absent, women are able to *adapt* by taking the man's position, and they begin to position themselves into survival mode and behave more masculine. Most of us would agree that men have a built-in honor code, while this is not necessarily inherent to women. Women will do whatever is necessary—fight, claw, and strategically position—to provide for themselves and their children. Women who lack the honor code can become ruthless at work, especially if a man has abandoned her by choice, she hasn't gotten help or found freedom from the abuse, or she doesn't have a handle on her anger.

My heart breaks for single mothers. Satan seems to work overtime to make them feel incomplete and wants them to work so hard and be so busy that they don't have as much time to spend with God, in His Word, or going to church. The enemy tells women lies, trying to convince them they don't have time for themselves or their friends, because he knows that encourages and strengthens them. While a woman's adaptability is powerful as she adapts to and thrives in different seasons in her life (single, married, widowed, etc.), the truth is she wasn't built to be able to carry what a man carries physically or mentally—she was wired differently.

4. Women bring forth life and beauty.

A woman's emotional makeup and ability to bring forth life and beauty is something powerful that God put into her. It seems God gave females the nurturing, compassionate, tender, creative side of His character. (While men also have these qualities, women express them more easily and frequently than men.) God chose to give a woman the ability to conceive life, birth life, and speak life into a baby as it develops inside of her. The birthing experience not only changes her physically but emotionally and spiritually as well.

It's important to note in this key that Satan despises anyone or anything that produces *life*, because it thwarts his evil plan. He is a thief and his mode of operation is *death*, the very *opposite of life.* John 10:10 (NKJV) says, "The thief does not come except to steal, and to kill, and to destroy. I have come that they may have life, and that they may have it more abundantly." Satan focuses on the spiritual power and influence God has given to His children. He is relentless in his attacks on their potential and the potential they see in others. He uses a female's sensitivity to taunt women with threats toward her, her children, her husband, and those she cherishes. He hates all God's children because they reflect His image, but it's quite possible he targets women more fiercely than men. Oh, don't get me wrong, Satan hates men, but he *especially hates women* because they are designed to bring forth life, and *he knows* what a new life can do to his kingdom of darkness. He sees when men are not in their position (just like in the Garden of Eden) and women are unprotected, making them easy prey. Satan uses whomever he can to hurt women, so when he can get an unsuspecting male who is important to her to take up his assignment, he can hurt both of them *and* God's heart. He knows he might devour and destroy generations if he can just get her off track or, better yet, destroy her completely. (We'll dig deeper into this in Chapter 7.)

5. Women monitor their environments because environments speak to them.

Environments constantly *speak* to females. (Men have told me this is one of the keys that surprised them as much as learning about the "female fear factor," and understanding it changed their lives dramatically.) To a man, the environment inside and outside of the home is quiet, but to a woman, if she is awake, the environment is *loud!*

Women hear:

- The dishes say, "Wash me."

- The bed says, "Make me."
- The socks on the floor say, "Put me in the laundry."
- The grocery list says, "Buy me."
- The baby says, "Feed me."
- The neighbor says, "Come meet me."
- The school says, "Come help us."
- The parent says, "Come visit me."
- The church says, "Bring a meal to a hurting family."
- The Sunday school class says, "Come teach me."
- The friend says, "Come have lunch with me."
- The toddler says, "Come play with me."
- The lunch boxes say, "Fill me."
- The dinner says, "Plan and cook me."
- The bills say, "Pay me."
- The car says, "Fill me and wash me."
- The husband says, "Come pay attention to me."
- The mirror says, "Lose some weight."
- The hair says, "Cut me."
- The laundry says, "Fold me."

Are you getting the idea?! (The women who are reading this right now are nodding their heads "Yes," while the men are scratching theirs!)

It's true! Environments inside and outside of the home speak to females of all ages. Again, God may have put this into her so she can care for children, multitask, and "collect and connect" effectively, but when things get out of balance, it can be destructive to her.

Men, if you need her undivided attention or want her to focus on you or something you want to tell her, take her to a place in the house where nothing needs her attention or care.

I think this key explains why it is important for women to get time alone to take a bubble bath, read a book, watch a movie, or have lunch with girlfriends. Healthy women offer healthy conversation. Women need relationships that give and take almost in equal portions, so when women are together they don't just care for one another, *they get cared for too.*

So, guys whether it's a simple conversation or sexual intimacy, remember that women need to be in an environment that's not vying for her attention. Create a quiet atmosphere for her. For a man, sex makes everything right but for most women, she doesn't want to have sex *until* everything *seems* right. So, guys help her quiet the environment if you want her to be able to give her undivided attention to you. That means the kids are settled and asleep, the dishes are done, and the laundry's put away. I've heard it said for years that "sex begins in the kitchen." I think it's true! If men want women to have energy for them, they need to help her bring order to her environment and quiet things down visually and emotionally.

Most men think she expects a romantic, candlelit dinner with him gazing into her eyes speaking sentences as poems, while holding both of her hands. Honestly, she might get a little suspicious. (Ha!) But, taking her to a small restaurant that is quiet and dimly lit, with a tablecloth and soothing music will turn her radar down. She would love to be the object of your affection and will feel safe and anchored if you will just touch her periodically. This quiet, safe atmosphere will allow her to emotionally connect with you, which can lead to physical connection later. If a female is just going through the motions with her radar spinning at full speed, sex just becomes another duty for her and her mind and heart are not in it.

6. Women constantly hear the accusing voice of the enemy.

Most women concur they constantly battle with an inner voice of condemnation, competition, and comparison. Ask a woman what she's *not* good at and she will quickly rattle off a list. Men, on the other hand, don't usually focus on their weaknesses. The voice inside of women probably originated in the Garden of Eden and comes from the enemy of our soul (mind, will, and emotions)—Satan. His voice often sounds very familiar to her because it may have begun the moment she took her first breath. **Current culture only amplifies the voice of perfection for women today, and these voices may have become shouts for Christian women. I call it the voice of the "perfect Christian woman." Satan is such a thief and liar! (John 8:44)**

Many women know intellectually they are made in the image of God and are loved and valued, but deep down, few really *believe* it because they are so hard on themselves. The media, which is propelled by the enemy, only turns up the volume as she ages. Daily, she sees and hears messages like, "You're too fat, thin, tall, short, light, or dark." "Look at *her*. She's so much prettier, smarter, and more put together than you are!" "Look at those magazines; why can't you look more like *her*?"

"What's wrong with *you*?" "Buy this, buy that, and you'll look more like her." "He would have stayed with you (and the kids) if you were *enough*." "You lost that job because you aren't as pretty, smart, or available as _____." "Act more like a man, and you'll get the next promotion." It's *never ending!* Women know this voice. If you don't believe me, just ask any woman if it's true.

7. Women need heroes in their lives.

A woman without a leader feels exposed. Women need heroes as much as the men in their lives need to be heroes. God designed women to need what men were designed to give: strong, confident, tender, trustworthy heroes to cover, cherish, and lead them.

Men, a leader's best role model is Jesus. If you have a desire to learn more about women while knowing God through His Word, the Holy Spirit will partner with you and develop the hero in you at breakneck speed. A true hero not only brings confidence and strength to a woman but to an entire family or organization. One thing men can be sure of is this: Women are always looking for a hero, and if you do not provide that for her, she will find one, even if she steps into the position herself!

8. Women monitor the happiness of the men in their lives.

For a woman, monitoring her surroundings begins very early in life and is something she never seems to outgrow.

Even as a little girl, a female knows the covering of a man, in most cases her daddy or someone standing in for him such as a close relative, is imperative to her health, safety, and well-being. It is wired into her fragile, little heart. She needs to know he's there and willing to provide for and protect her. It's part of her DNA.

Women also have an innate need to be cherished and pleasing to the men in their lives. A woman will monitor a man who is important to her when she is in his presence *because* she wants him to be happy with her. She believes if he's happy with her and values her that he will be at his post providing and protecting her. **To a male, female monitoring may sometimes seem like she is being overly controlling, but it's her need for protection that drives her.** Just knowing he is pleased with her makes her feel secure.

Guys, here is a clue for future reference: If you ever wonder what a woman in your presence is thinking, she is almost always thinking, even if unconsciously, "*Is he pleased with me? If he's not, he may not protect me!* For most women, monitoring men who are important to them while they are in their presence continues throughout their life. Personally, this was very freeing for me to learn, because I thought it was a flaw. I now know it's the way God made me!

9. **Women need time alone to putter, arrange, connect, and be creative.**

Most men don't see this because it usually happens when women are alone. Periodically a woman will walk through her home or office alone, moving, relocating, touching, and organizing. It is a way she can *connect* with what she has *collected*. Guys don't always understand this behavior, and really, women don't either, but they do it more often than they realize.

When a woman is alone at home for a long period, such as when her husband goes out of town, she has more time to focus because she has no one to monitor. Her need to bring forth color and beauty may cause a sudden rush of creativity. Some women may choose to cook, sew, plant, paint, refurbish furniture, or just move through the house repositioning or rearranging things. She may gather supplies, prepare a space just for herself, get her favorite snacks, and organize "her" environment *her way*. She feels free to just "be." In a few hours she may become aware that no one is there to provide for or protect *her*, and her creative (feminine) side may begin to slow down. Her more masculine self rises up, as she has to move into the role of protector and provider. She is on duty. This shift will slowly drain the creativity out of her as she begins to step into a more masculine way of being. She will check to be sure all the doors are locked, walk the dog (outside in the dark), and begin to do things the man in her life usually does. It helps that women are wired to be highly adaptable.

When a man is about to step back into his position of provider and protector after being away, it is helpful if he calls her and lets her know he is on his way back into the atmosphere. This can help the transition for both of them to be less abrupt. Unless a rhythm is found and grace is given (on both sides), the reentry process may be difficult and even destructive. However, the transition can be mastered with focus, communication, sensitivity, and desire.

● ● ●

I watched this swing routinely with my dad, who was an airline pilot, and my stay-at-home mom. When my dad was on a trip, my mom would sew like crazy! She made all the clothing my sister and I wore when we were growing up. (I appreciate her for that now more now than ever!) She and my dad shared a sewing room/study. So when dad was out on a trip, their shared space became her sewing room. She would rarely come out of the sewing room because the clock was ticking and her creative time in there alone was limited. As soon as she knew the jet's front tires had hit the runway, she would begin to change and transition, because her responsibilities changed radically when he was back at his post. She could no longer just be where she wanted to be without monitoring my dad.

When Dad retired, it was a tough transition for her. She felt she lost her freedom because she was subconsciously monitoring my dad all the time. It wasn't his fault; it was just that the rhythm had changed. For 33 years, he'd left her for three days at time, and she had grown accustomed to having alone time. Now the balance was off and she was monitoring all the time. It takes work to find a rhythm and balance, but knowing this key helps make the transition easier.

10. Women need purpose and someone or something to love.

Females are wired for purpose and will always find one. I believe a woman's first purpose is to love. The Bible *commands* husbands to love their wives. It urges women to love their husbands, but nowhere does it *command* women to love them. I believe that's because it's more natural for women to love—that's how God wired them!

Females will always find *something* or *someone* to pour love into. Even little girls look for purpose by loving, nurturing, and playing house with their dolls or lining up their stuffed animals pretending they are her students and she is the teacher. Single women may find their purpose in being a student, developing a career path, being in ministry, or caring for friends and family. A widow may find purpose in leading a Bible study, volunteering, or holding a job. Because God wired women with a need to collect and connect, whether they're married, in a serious relationship, or single, they will find much of their purpose associated with family and people they're in relationship with. Women also need to produce beauty, either physically (in her environment) or emotionally (in people and relationships).

The first priority for married men and women in God's economy is the ministry of the home and the people in it. Godly women learn to create a safe, organized environment of peace for their children and, most importantly, their husbands. Everyone needs a place of refuge from the storms of life, a place where they feel accepted, nurtured, and loved. The world will beat us up, but women can offer a place of safety within the walls of the home, but only when it is *safe for her and she feels protected.*

It is beneficial for a woman to be covered by a man who not only understands her need for *purpose and love* but also helps her achieve it. When men appreciate the fact that she is using her God-given gifts *for him* and those in their family or organization, it causes her to thrive. It is a beautiful thing when a man provides and protects and a woman gets to collect, connect, and use and enjoy what he has so graciously provided for her.

● ● ●

Because of our culture, a woman's purpose, especially when she doesn't work outside of the home, is hard to define. Stay-at-home moms have the most important job on the planet, yet sadly, it's the least respected in most circles. I was shocked even 20 years ago when I would go to a business function with Don and both men and women would ask me what I did. When I said, "I am a mom, and a wife," they would quickly snap their heads in the opposite direction and ask the next female what she did. It was shocking. I don't think they meant to be cruel; they just didn't know exactly how to respond. I have to admit it was discouraging. I had a degree and had built and run a successful business, but now because I chose to stay at home, it seemed I was perceived to have less value.

Staying at home did not seem to pay very well at the time, but let me just say, now that those babies are adults, the rewards are greater than I ever imagined. I will admit, after having my own business and my own "extra cash," it was scary to completely depend upon Don. I wasn't used to that. God more than honored our decision for me to stay home and raise our kids. It was often overwhelming because I had not gone to school to learn how to be a mom, and I had no idea what I was doing most of the time! God's grace is sufficient when we depend on Him. Thank goodness He continued to pursue me, teach me, and lead me! His promises are true and being a stay-at-home mom was a huge privilege.

11. Women need emotional and verbal approval.

Emotionally, women are connected to the mood and/or attitudes of the men in their lives. Because women have the ability to adapt, a man's mood has the ability to change a woman's feelings because it changes her environment. If a man in her life (husband, boyfriend, father, brother, boss, etc.) seems to be in a bad mood, bothered, or discontent, she will try (even subconsciously) to find out what's wrong and make it better. Because it's important for her to have peace in her environment, whether it's at the office or at home, she has a desire to make things better and bring harmony to the world around her and the people in it.

Men: It may be hard for you to understand this but almost 100% of the time when you are in a bad mood, the women in your life (both at work and at home) will automatically assume it's because of something she did. This probably seems ridiculous to you but just assume it's true. She is very sensitive to your moods so when you don't say anything, it further perpetuates this assumption.

It's important for men to pay attention to a woman's mood swings. If a woman senses the men in her world are not pleased, her "pleaser radar" goes into high gear, and she begins to swing from one thing to the next, trying different approaches to make them pleased and happy with her. (Of course this, apart from the Lord, can develop into codependency.) Because women are wired to adapt, it's easy for them to change their approach to try to please men. If men see the pendulum swinging out of control, what she is saying is, "Do you see me? Can you hear me? Am I important to you? Are you pleased with me? Are you still going to protect me?" It's important for men to pay attention and make eye contact with her and communicate if they're upset, if it has nothing to do with her. Men should find a way to let a woman know when it's not her fault. And if it is something she did, he should share it in a tender, considerate way understanding she "wants" him to be happy with her and at his post. When men miss pendulum swings, women have a tendency to become more needy and less secure.

Verbally, women need to hear they have the approval of important men in their lives. Just as men's tanks are fueled by women's happiness and gratitude, women's tanks are fueled by men's ability to make her feel cherished and precious to him through his attitudes, actions, and words of gratitude. **When men follow the example of Christ and treat women with the same respect Christ treats His bride (the Church), they thrive.** It's important for men to courageously reach out, connect with women, and build them up. Honest conversations can aide bringing trust, but remember, **a woman is highly sensitive to the criticism of a man who doesn't ever build her up.** If a man builds up the woman (or women and girls) in his life, she will want to hear what he has to say because she is wired to want to please him. When she sees men in her life who are trustworthy, she will do all she can to bring harmony and unity to those relationships. Women who are built up with encouraging words are more confident and, in turn, are more honoring and supportive to the men in their lives.

● ● ●

Husbands, your wife needs to know she is the most beautiful girl in the world to you. If you don't tell her she looks pretty, then it doesn't matter what anyone else thinks. She needs to hear it from the most important man in her world. If a wife believes she can't please her husband, her insecurity may eventually drive her to another man she feels she can please, if only temporarily.

In the early years of our marriage before I became a Christian, I stepped dangerously close to the edge of this pit. Because of Don's background, he was emotionally shut off from me. I couldn't get him to "see me." I was working full-time, running my design firm. While I didn't have a physical affair with another man, my mind was completely involved with him in an emotional affair. Satan had his laser pointed at the wound in my heart and my loneliness made me *extremely* susceptible. He tried to convince me another man could offer me everything my husband couldn't at the time.

Watch out men and women! Satan is a liar and circles overhead watching for the wounded to begin to limp, lag behind, and wander off alone. He is poised and ready, and weak men and women have his focus and attention. Satan will send an experienced vulture, dressed to look like the ticket out, but really "the ticket" has come to devour you and your family (present *and* future).

Thankfully, Jesus was focused on my situation too, and He came and gave me a way out! I look back at that time and realize I was flying *way too close* to the fire; it's a miracle I didn't get incinerated. I am often reminded of what my rebellion could have cost me if I had continued. I would never have known two of the greatest gifts of my life, Jonathan and Holly.

12. Women overtalk when they feel insecure.

When a woman feels nervous, devalued, unprotected, or exposed, she becomes insecure and has a tendency to "overtalk." Insecurity in a woman leads to intimidation and makes her feel vulnerable. In turn, this causes her to act out, often in fear, by talking incessantly. In reality, it's just a defense mechanism women use when they feel insecure, unimportant, and invisible or like they don't measure up.

• • •

Because I was wounded, out of balance, and intensely insecure, which could have been compounded by the fact that I was a stay-at-home mom and starving for adult conversation, I was a woman who overtalked (and still can be if I don't stay alert). Don used to make fun of me because he did not understand why I was like this. He used to be very quiet and introverted, which would sometimes embarrass me, and I felt I needed to make up for what I saw as "Don's arrogance." (I now know it was Don's insecurity manifesting, not his arrogance.) When we were with people and I felt nervous, I would begin talking incessantly. This would lead Don to comment sarcastically to those around us, "She breathes through her ears." This made me talk more! Now that he knows why, he doesn't think it's funny because he realizes my talking was a reflection of how unsafe I felt when I was with him. This key of truth has been a tremendous help to us.

Guys, if a woman in your life is overly talkative, you might want to ask the Lord why she's overtalking. She may feel exposed, unprotected, and insecure, and you may be the person she is protecting herself from. Make an effort to emotionally cover and validate her and see what happens.

13. Women can be anchored by a man's non-sexual touch.

Touch is very powerful to a woman. When a trustworthy husband touches a woman in a non-sexual way by holding her hand, touching her arm or her knee, or putting his hand on the small of her back, it centers and calms her *immediately*. It lets her know he is there for her, focused on her, and ready to provide for and protect her. Because men are single focused, a woman highly values any effort he expresses by making her the object of his focus through touch. Whether driving down the road, walking through the kitchen, strolling through a shopping area, or reaching across the table at dinner to hold her hand, a woman feels anchored and settles in when a man touches her. She loves to know he is present emotionally and physically there to protect her. Even a look into her eyes from across a room lets a woman know he is available, aware of her, and she is important to him.

A touch, however, is *not a substitution for an emotional and verbal connection*. When a touch is used in place of emotional or verbal intimacy (or out of habit), one of two things may happen: (1) She may feel a void, which will cause her to question the authenticity of the man, and she may eventually feel manipulated. (2) She may grow used to the habitual touch and cease to crave emotional or verbal intimacy, causing her to disconnect emotionally. This can lead to her becoming very independent or cause her to look for another person to connect with intellectually, emotionally, or spiritually.

14. Women need to feel nurtured and cherished.

A woman feels most cherished and nurtured when she is free to be her feminine self and has a trustworthy man who is available and anxious to hold her. The best way to describe this is when a husband holds a woman close to his chest with his left arm around her shoulders and his right arm fully extended with his sword drawn to protect her against anything that would come her way. Regardless of the continent or culture, *every* woman is designed to desire *this* position. It's in this position physically and emotionally that she finds all other expressions of being nurtured and cherished.

A man's strength should not be used to threaten or overpower a woman but to care for, nurture, cherish, and cover her. A woman who is not nurtured by a man may close her heart to him, isolate herself, and become silent around him. This can bring a sense of oppression, which can lead to depression, desperation, and defensiveness. The deeper she slides into the hole, the more work and time will be required to coax her out.

● ● ●

I've had the extreme privilege of taking this message to Tokyo, Japan. I wondered if these keys would translate and cross cultural lines, but after I shared, it was clear they truly are universal.

A wife needs a husband to nurture her by showing gentleness and understanding even when she is undeserving (just as Christ does with his bride, the Church). A husband who gently washes her with words God gives him *for* her will eventually get a great return for his effort. **When a man is in the Word and listening to the Lord, the words he speaks over his wife bring power and life.** Ephesians 5:25–28 (MSG) says, "Husbands, go all out in your love for your wives, exactly as Christ did for the church—a love marked by giving, not getting. Christ's love makes the church whole. His words evoke her beauty. Everything he does and says is designed to bring the best out of her, dressing her in dazzling white silk, radiant with holiness. And that is how husbands ought to love their wives. They're really doing themselves a favor—since they're already 'one' in marriage." When married men live by this truth, they have the awesome privilege of presenting their bride's soul and spirit back to the Father in heaven in beautiful condition.

15. **Women are more likely to submit to a man who walks in a balance of humility and authority.**

A man (husband, boss, or ministry leader) who operates with an authentic and consistent balance of authority and humility brings a great sense of security to the women around him. When a man aligns himself with the Lord, his heart and attitudes change and women begin to trust his direction and yield to his authority with ease. A woman thrives in this type of environment, and it allows her to become vulnerable, lay down her sword, and become who God created her to be.

Conversely, women find it difficult to be vulnerable and submissive to *prideful men* who are in authority. Men who wield authority with little to no humility bring out fear and insecurity in women. Women who know God and His character understand that "God opposes the proud but gives grace to the humble" (James 4:6). Pride is really a form of *self-worship*. Pride is evident in someone who is not yielded to God and wants his or her own way. They think they know best and are always right. A godly woman fears submitting to a prideful man, because she knows pride is a sin and sin never affects just one person—*it affects the entire family or organization.* When men humble themselves and partner with women, it brings safety and security. If men don't humble themselves, the Lord will have no choice but to humble them. **The greatest gift a man can give his family is to follow the example of Christ and lead as a kind shepherd and a responsible king.** When he doesn't, her fear may cause her to eventually pull away *or* shut down emotionally to protect herself from him. This is a very destructive downward spiral!

Submit to one another out of reverence for Christ.
Ephesians 5:21 (NIV)

Every family or organization needs a leader who has authority, but **true authority comes with great responsibility.** God put men in a position to cover, support, and partner with women, not to dominate or control them. A strong leader offers safety by taking responsibility and leading the team or family. The person responsible must be given the authority they need to have the power to lead. It's important to remember **God designed submission as a place of safety for both men and women**, but for women it is vital because of the way they are physically built. Healthy women recognize that submission is something they are wired by God to desire. It is not scary, but rather safe when a leader is walking with a balance of humility and authority.

Women who walk in submission to authority set an example to their daughters and help create a desire in their sons for a woman like her. Likewise, how a man leads and treats his wife and daughters models for his sons the value (or lack of value) he has for women. (This is the same for men who work with women. How they behave toward the women they work with is an example to his male employees and colleagues.) When women, specifically wives and daughters, are not protected, nurtured, treated tenderly, and considered more fragile by men, they may become like one of the guys, just trying to survive. A woman will often become independent and behave in a more masculine way if her husband is not taking his position as the leader. Men have a wonderful opportunity to train their sons and daughters by modeling the value of femininity toward his wife. **When men treat women as God intended, it brings out the best in everyone and brings balance to the home and workplace.**

Men, before you step into the position of provider, protector, and coverer, you must choose to trust and obey the Lord. Remember, you are wired to take your position as a mighty warrior, dependable hunter, and responsible king. Through the sanctification process, you will also become a loving, tender shepherd. When you're courageous enough to reposition and partner with God *for* her, she will more than likely be more vulnerable and let you lead. She aches for this! However, in order to do so, you must first learn to rest in the arms of the heavenly Father. Even if you didn't have a Christ-like earthly father, you have a heavenly father who's desperate to love you and show you the way. Jesus is the perfect example of a priest and king. Study His example in the Bible, then pray and ask Him to show you what He sees about your leadership style and what He wants you to speak over the women in your life to build them up and encourage them. Allow Him to strengthen and train you so you can become a godly leader to those He has placed under your care. Take your God-ordained position with humility and see how it affects the males *and* females in your world.

You're cheating on God. If all you want is your own way, flirting with the world every chance you get, you end up enemies of God and his way. And do you suppose God doesn't care? The proverb has it that "he's a fiercely jealous lover." And what he gives in love is far better than anything else you'll find. It's common knowledge that "God goes against the willful proud; God gives grace to the willing humble."
James 4:4–6 (MSG)

16. Women need emotional intimacy; flowers, romantic dinners, gifts, and trips are of enormous value, but are not a substitute.

A woman needs to know the important man in her life cares and wants to connect with her. Flowers, gifts, romantic dinners, and trips say, "I am thinking of you," but they are just the icing on the cake. The quality of the cake is more important than the icing. If a cake is decorated beautifully, it can be especially disappointing if the inside is like cardboard. Beautiful decoration is not supposed to cover up something dry and flavorless inside. When a man does give gifts, she needs to know he thought of her just because, not because it's an expected holiday or because he wants to get out of the doghouse. Women need men who will emotionally step into their world and connect with them by listening, asking about their feelings, and sharing their feelings with them.

● ● ●

One Thanksgiving not too long ago, Don and I decided to go on our first trip in years without the kids. (It was our year to have the kids and their spouses for Christmas, which meant they were not with us for Thanksgiving.) Don really wanted to go on a cruise, but I was nervous about how we would be around one another on a ship without any distractions for *seven days*. We hadn't been on a trip alone (no business associates, friends, family, or kids) since our honeymoon, let alone on a cruise in the middle of the ocean. No Internet. No work. No friends. *Just us!* I must admit I had fear of discovering our emotional healing was not as deep as I thought it was *What if Don disconnected like he had for years? Would we cease to talk, and just sit on the balcony awkwardly staring at the rolling waves? Now that kids are grown, married, and settled in their individual lives independent from us, would we still have something to talk about? Would he still be able to focus on me or would he hurt my feelings?* We'd come so far, I was afraid of a setback. I knew the trip could be a huge blessing *or* it could be a waste of time and money and do a lot of emotional damage to both of us. Honestly, just a few years ago, I would not have had the courage to have taken the trip with just Don. Thankfully, because of the keys of truth and because we have taken the time to connect with and understand one another, we had a wonderful time and found that we were more connected than ever. Now we've learned to appreciate our differences and give each other grace, we don't take things so personally, and we enjoy being lovers *and* friends. We've learned whether we're with people or alone in the middle of the ocean, *we get each other.* Our time alone on the cruise made us want to do it again, and soon!

17. Women withhold emotionally and verbally when they don't feel safe.

Most women only share emotionally with people they trust. When a woman ceases to communicate (with men or women), it may mean she doesn't trust the person or has, for some reason, felt a need to disconnect from them emotionally.

If a man or woman was to ask a female, "How was your day?" and she says, "Fine." Then they ask, "Were you busy at work or was it slow?" And she responds with a short answer such as, "It was normal," that's a good sign she doesn't feel safe or there is something wrong. **A female almost always takes time to give details, because she is wired to *connect* with people.** Warm, connected conversation usually includes details and descriptions (of good and bad situations) about her day at work. It's a good sign when men invite women to share, and *they share and share and share and share.* It means she feels safe.

Men, if someone asked you what you did on Saturday, you would probably answer, "I went to Home Depot." If someone asked a female the same question and she *trusted* the person asking, she would give a "collection report." She would list each errand she ran, who she saw, what they talked about, and how it made her feel. So, how can you help her? Remember she is collecting and connecting with pieces of information all day. It's in her nature to collect them and then pour over the pieces she has collected and try to make something beautiful out of them. Collectors constantly take visual pictures and remember the areas they have been collecting so they can revisit the good experiences again. Men are the opposite. Men take notes of places to hide and wait because they are hunting or positioning for battle. Guys, you will benefit greatly if you recognize the opportunity to offer to *hold the handle of her pitcher and let her pour.* Even if you don't understand or necessarily care about what she is sharing, or if it doesn't make sense to you, love her enough and be understanding enough to let her pour. The longer you let her pour, the more room she will have for you!

When a man seems discontent, disconnected, depressed, or disengaged with the woman (or women) in his life, she may try desperately to get him to re-engage and be happy. Over time, if she can't make him happy or get him to connect, she may begin to lose her "*voice*" (her belief that what she *says* has value), and if it continues, she may eventually lose her sense of "true self" (her belief that she has *any* value to him at all). When women lose their voice, something inside of them dies. Because women are wired to connect, communication is very important to their emotional and physical health. If she believes she has lost her voice, she will eventually believe she has lost her God-given influence and power. When a woman stays in this emotional place for very long, she may eventually get physically ill. Her soul (mind, will, and emotions) becomes sick. Her ability to bring color and life into her family and world diminishes dramatically. Not being able to use her voice to speak life (into her family), give input, or have influence causes a female to slowly die from the inside out. Because men are not wired with or for the same purpose, this may be a hard concept for them to comprehend. Yet it is important for men to understand that this is a scary place for a woman and can completely immobilize her.

18. Women assume men are withholding information when they are not communicating.

A female often assumes when a man doesn't share *details* he is withholding information from her. Women assume when men don't give details it's because he is either disinterested or, for some unknown reason, angry. She may even go so far as to believe he is punishing her, because this is what women tend to do when they are not verbally connecting. **A woman often believes whatever is going on to cause his silence is her fault, so she tries to fix it.** So what's crazy about this? Her assumption is usually wrong, because it has nothing to do with her. A man may be preoccupied with something that happened at work or something completely unrelated to her. Oftentimes a man has no idea she is overreacting *because she thinks it is her fault.* The truth is, in most cases, men don't talk because they don't have anything to say. His mind may be focused on something else or, amazingly, he may be thinking about or focused on absolutely *nothing*! (It's strange to a woman, but men's brains are capable of being in neutral and thinking about nothing!) Allowing a man time to be still and quiet is a gift *to him*. (Remember ladies, he isn't built like you; he doesn't have continuous radar that never stops, like you do.) When a man lets a woman know he just wants to be quiet and it's not personal, it's a gift *to her*.

Men, if a woman asks you to go get something for her at the grocery store, she will probably try to give you lots of specifics you really don't think you need, because she's trying to help you. She may even tell you the specific aisle and shelf the breakfast bars are on as well as the color and design of the box. It's important to remember she does this because she is trying help you by making it easier for you. She forgets you like to *hunt* for things.

Men, it can be very hurtful and destructive if you interrupt and cut her off. She is wired to give details, but if you shut her down by saying, "I've got it!" what she hears is, "I don't need your information. I know more than you do. You are weak and may not be worth protecting." I know it sounds strange and it may be hard for you to believe, but most women really feel this way whether they can articulate it or not. To her, if you don't think what she says is important, she starts to feel like you may not value her enough to protect her, and that scares her. This is one of the reasons women may blow things out of proportion. Men, remember, women can multiply everything, good and bad.

Another reminder men, when you communicate, sometimes you *omit* details that you don't feel need any explanation, but that is not always sufficient from a woman's point of view. She may want more details, not because she is snooping or trying to control you but because she is looking for a point of connection with you.

19. **Women need female friendship to be healthy and whole and to relieve men from the need to be something they can't be.**

Women need *girlfriends*. Not just any girlfriends, but friendships with girls who *give* and *take* in almost equal portions. They need healthy community with friends who are both older and younger. **A woman needs to pour *and* be poured into.** She needs friends who fill her up and don't deplete her. Healthy women need other healthy women in their lives in order to stay healthy and emotionally alive because they are constantly *pouring out*.

This is a very important part of a woman's world. While men usually don't need this like women do, it is wise and can benefit a man when he recognizes the women in his life need this and helps them achieve it. It is also important for women to understand it's not fair to a man when they try to force him to be what *only a girlfriend* can be, because, try as he may, he can't ever fill that role.

Warning! Women, because of your inborn radar as well as your desire to love and be loved, you need to be careful not fall into a trap of (1) being drawn only to people who need you; and (2) becoming enablers to people who need to learn to trust the Lord (instead of humans). When we continue to rescue and enable others, we get in the way of allowing God to teach them to know Him better and trust Him more. God wants us to be sensitive to one another's needs, but be careful not to let those needs pull us away from our time with God or our first ministry (home and family), as that becomes dangerous (to you and your family). It's sad to see the enemy take the very gifts God has given you *for Him* and use them to make you empty and exhausted.

This is something I had to learn the hard way. Thinking I was being a "good Christian," I unintentionally let some people suck the life out of me. I thought I was simply ministering to hurting people, but instead we were both becoming co-dependent on one another. This happens when we feel too responsible for the health and happiness of others. I allowed my brokenness to drive me to help others, because I got something out of it. It was very dangerous for me and for those I thought I was helping. Jesus calls us to love people, but sometimes we get confused about *what love really is*, and it can become enabling. That's not love. Ministering to people can feel energizing at first, but when out of balance, *it's dangerous*. I learned it could also create a need and an appetite in me to be needed, which would often cause me to be distracted from the Savior and my family. Again, Satan is a thief, and he works in our weaknesses and unhealed wounds!

When we have our eyes on the wrong thing, it often feeds our pride. Far too many well-intentioned Christian women with pure motives (especially in the beginning of their walk with Jesus) fall into this trap and become addicted to doing "good" and being "needed." It is not healthy, nor is it the way the Lord intended us to use our gifts. He wants us so close that we have our heads on His chest daily in our quiet time so we can identify His voice, hear His directives, and confidently obey.

20. **Women need men to partner with them, especially while raising children.**

Women need their children's fathers to be engaged in child rearing. When husbands are distracted (by work or outlets) or are not co-partnering with their wives, the kids often take advantage of their mothers. When men are not *physically* or *emotionally* present, it can be the loneliest time in the world for women, especially during the child's adolescent years.

Raising teens can be a very lonely time for mothers, especially if the dad is gone a lot or emotionally disconnected. (This was one of the hardest times for me personally as a parent.) While babies can be *physically* demanding, teens can be *emotionally* demanding. During middle school and high school, kids can become entitled and selfish and emotionally drain their mom. If a dad is not supportive of her (and present physically, emotionally, and spiritually), the kids can deeply damage the mom, cause her to lose confidence, give up, and give in to the kids, which can end in disaster.

During this season, mothers see their children's potential, but at the same time, they struggle with fear that their children's immaturity may lead to bad choices and cause life-altering, negative consequences. (Men are *usually* oblivious to this.) **When the dad is absent physically or emotionally it can cause her "female fear factor" to shift into overdrive.**

This season of raising adolescent children can be bittersweet. A mom is *constantly* serving, giving, training, equipping, and monitoring *everyone* in the home, and she is never off duty. Her radar is running nonstop as she juggles and tries to balance responsibilities with her kids as well as her husband. If she is a Christian woman, she takes the job of raising godly children very seriously and, in this culture, it's *very* difficult. She knows Satan is a thief, and she needs help from Dad as she battles the forces of darkness that are so prevalent in the current world's system.

She is shifting, changing, and adapting, all while trying to loosen her heartstrings in preparation to launch each child out into the world. It can be very intense, and support from the children's dad as well as his emotional and physical presence is the anchor she needs to stay balanced. Of course, the Lord Jesus is the best anchor in this season, but God created us all to *need people* to help us to stay on track. The enemy's voice is loud to a mom during this time.

WARNING! Satan sets another trap for women with teens, especially for women whose husbands are not emotionally connected. It's the pitfall of becoming too enmeshed in their children's lives. Some women transfer their need to love and be loved to their teens. This can cause some women to try to win the approval of their kids by acting cool; they become too much like a friend to their kids. Children only have one mom and one dad. We have to be parents to them until they are adults and no longer need parenting. If we have done our part well, when our children become adults they will respect us, choose to be our friends, and come to us when they need advice or counsel. It's a sweet reward for parenting God's way. When we enable the children, they can become confused and handicapped, making it hard to leave, cleave, or spread their wings. If the individualization of the teen has not been allowed to flourish during their adolescent years, their growth will be stunted and boundaries may be hard to define. This will make it hard for the teen to differentiate and build a life of his or her own, making independence and marriage difficult.

21. **Women who receive unexplained "nos" tend to emasculate the men who made the decision, because they feel discounted.**

When decisions have to be made in a relationship or an organization, it really doesn't matter who makes more money. What matters is *who is responsible for the specific area in question and how they communicate the information.* If a husband or male boss or superior responds (in an area of their responsibility) with a "no," and takes time to explain the reason, it can create trust and value for a woman. If the "no" is sent down like a judge and jury without any explanation, women may cease to partner, and the team may be (invisibly) fractured.

Women feel bullied when a man, especially one who has a higher income than her, hands down an unexplained "no" because they feel men don't see them as a viable, equal team member. In response, a female may usurp his authority and emasculate the man who handed down the verdict as a defense mechanism because she is hurt, angry, frustrated, or frightened. Whether it's spending money or making decisions about the direction a family or company is going, *explaining* a "no" can build unity and bring validation to the family or team.

Men, if a decision (or a discussion) comes up within your area of responsibility and it really doesn't matter that much to you and won't break the budget, consider giving her the gift of a "yes." It will help build her confidence in you and help her follow you with trust, while strengthening your team.

For example, when we moved into our new home, Don was very excited about our back porch—or as he calls it now, his "man cave." He had TVs and electric shades installed so he could enclose it and watch football with the guys. The only problem is he had expectations and ideas for this space that he never shared with me. I, on the other hand, saw great potential to make it an extension of the house where we could both entertain and relax. I ordered a beautiful black rug with a bright floral design of red, turquoise, and yellow swirling through it. I bought beautiful floral pillows for the dining area and plain red and black pillows to accent the floral rug in the TV area. I finished it off with a few outdoor plants. I was so excited about our new rug and when it arrived, I could not wait for Don to carry it out to the back porch and help me unroll it. We brought it outside and as he began unrolling it, I squealed with delight, "Don't you just love it!?" He stared at the rug and flatly said, "I thought this was my man cave. I thought we would get a Dallas Cowboys rug." It felt shocking to me because I thought we were sharing the space and that a rug with a black background was masculine enough. He said he was only kidding, but I was not sure. Ultimately, he gave me the gift of a "yes," because *that* wasn't worth not making me happy. (He still teases me whenever people come over by telling them he really wanted a Dallas Cowboys rug!) Don knew how much it meant to me to make the porch pretty, and I am thankful for the gift of his "yes" this time!

22. Women carry their emotions deep within their core.

A woman's emotions come from deep within her. When a female feels deep emotion it will usually come out of her by way of a word or a noise. Whether it is joy, sadness, anxiety, or fear, she will often show it all over her face, and when it's extreme, she will almost always make a noise. Her emotions come from such a deep place in her heart that they resonate through her entire being. She may squeal or even jump. Some women put their hands over their mouths or up in the air. Some jump for joy or kneel on the ground, as if the emotion that began deep within has finally made its way out! The next time you go to a play or a movie and something deeply emotional or really exciting happens on the screen or the stage, listen carefully for the sounds that come out of the audience. More than likely, they're coming from women. You will definitely hear them, because **women are wired to *feel* deeply and respond with a sound.** Female animals even make noise when they are excited or attempting to scare off predators. When men pay attention to the facial expressions and sounds a woman makes, he's often able to see into her heart and know what she is feeling deep inside.

23. **Women who feel worthless may have emotional outbursts.**

Satan enjoys kicking women when they're down, because *he is ruthless and relentless.* His goal is to not only hurt or destroy women; he wants to shatter everyone connected to her in the process. Satan has been observing males and females from the beginning, and he knows women want to please the men who are supposed to protect and provide for them. He also knows women hide pain, rejection, and disappointment out of fear they will be displeasing to men. Satan strategizes so that when a woman least expects it, he does something to trigger the pain she has tried to ignore or keep covered deep in her heart. This is where the sudden outbursts often come from. Many times these outbursts shock her, because she has worked so hard to convince herself she is over it, has forgotten it, or has forgiven the one who hurt her. (More about this in Chapter 7.)

24. **Women feel devalued by men who raise their voice.**

Men can take their strength for granted, and when they raise their voices, it can shatter a woman's feminine heart. She will disconnect emotionally, remove herself from the situation, or become a "masculinized" defender. When a man raises his voice, it causes a woman to feel devalued, disrespected, discounted, unprotected, and exposed, and she may eventually come out swinging her sword *at him*. If men pay attention, they can see the damage on a woman's face when they raise their voices. (More about this in Chapter 7.)

25. Women are crushed when their husbands or boyfriends look at or lust after other women.

It breaks a woman's heart when a man looks at or lusts after another woman (or women). It makes the woman he's with feel inadequate and unimportant. Regardless of what she may or may not say, it's cruel, rips her heart apart, destroys her trust in him, and wounds her to the core because she feels she is not only inferior but also left alone and exposed. It is not only destructive to her, but it sets a horrible example for their children. To his daughter it says, "You probably won't ever be enough," and to his son it says, "This is what men do. We can have whatever we want." Both are lies from Satan and can destroy hearts and lives. **Dads have a small window of opportunity to establish and model the value of women to their daughters and sons (or any children watching).** It's sad when children pick up bad behaviors from their home environment and develop core lies that can bring pain for generations.

● ● ●

Years ago the Lord spoke to my heart and said, "Be sure you are raising your children in a way you will enjoy watching when it's repeated, because you will see it all again." Now *that's* a sobering thought! God takes relationships and parenting very seriously, and we should too.

PAUSE, PONDER, PRAY, AND OBEY

MEN:

1. How do you feel about the keys of truth about women?

2. Where did your beliefs about women and their roles come from? Are these beliefs in line with God's design? Are there any lies you have believed about women?

3. Are there areas where you have not taken your position and provided for and protected the women in your life? If so, what are they?

4. Are there any women you need to apologize to and ask for forgiveness? If so, make a list and a plan to begin the process.

5. Did any of the keys about women surprise you? If so, which ones?

6. Did you learn anything new about women?

7. Which key of truth about women is most helpful to you?

8. Which keys do you need more clarity and understanding about? Ask the Lord to give you the clarity and understanding you need.

9. What do you sense the Lord wants you to do with what you've just learned, if anything?

10. Are you willing to reposition? If so, what is the first action you need to take to begin?

11. Pray and ask the Lord to help you see women from His perspective.

12. Pray and ask the Lord for the courage to step up and be the kind of man He made you to be by taking your position for the women in your life at home and work.

WOMEN:

1. How do you feel about the keys of truth about women?

2. Where did your beliefs about women and their roles come from? Are these beliefs in line with God's design? Are there any lies you have believed?

3. Did any of the keys about women surprise you? If so, which ones?

4. What did you learn about yourself that you didn't know?

5. Which keys do you relate to most? Why?

6. Which keys are most helpful to you? Why?

7. Are there any keys you can't relate to or that don't apply to you? If so, which ones are they, and why do you think that is?

8. Which keys do you need more clarity and understanding about? Ask the Lord to give you the clarity and understanding you need.

9. When was the last time you felt fear? How did you respond?

10. Are there any areas where you have adapted and become more masculine than you realized? If so, what areas are they and what do you want to do differently?

11. Are there any areas where you have shut down?

12. What do you sense the Lord wants you to do with what you've just learned, if anything?

13. Are you willing to reposition? If so, what is the first action you need to take to begin?

14. Pray and ask the Lord to help you see yourself from His perspective.

MEN AND WOMEN:

For the next few days or weeks, observe the females around you:

- How do women respond when they feel fear?
- How do they respond when they feel provided for and protected?

Listen to what they say, watch their faces and body language, and make notes.

• • •

There are three desires essential to a female's heart:

1. She yearns to be fought for (wanted and pursued).
2. She wants an adventure to share (she doesn't want to be the adventure).
3. She wants to have beauty to unveil (to be the beauty a man delights in).

Adapted from *Captivating* by John and Stasi Eldredge[13]

What is the Holy Spirit saying to you? Take some time to find three scripture verses that encourage you or confirm what you are hearing.

_____

_____

_____

_____

_____

_____

_____

_____

_____

_____

_____

_____

_____

_____

_____

_____

_____

_____

_____

_____

_____

_____

_____

_____

_____

_____

_____

_____

And He said to me, "My grace is sufficient for you, for My strength is made perfect in weakness." Therefore most gladly I will rather boast in my infirmities, that the power of Christ may rest upon me.
2 Corinthians 12:9 (NKJV)

For you did not receive the spirit of bondage again to fear, but you received the Spirit of adoption by whom we cry out, "Abba, Father."
Romans 8:15 (NKJV)

I beseech you therefore, brethren, by the mercies of God, that you present your bodies a living sacrifice, holy, acceptable to God, which is your reasonable service. And do not be conformed to this world, but be transformed by the renewing of your mind, that you may prove what is that good and acceptable and perfect will of God.
Romans 12:1–2 (NKJV)

Chapter 7

THE POWER OF
RESTORATION

A few years ago, Don and I had the scary but awesome privilege of traveling to Greece on a mission trip with a small team from our church. We went to support Christine Caine's ministry, The A21 Campaign, which is a non-profit, non-governmental organization that works to fight human trafficking, including sexual exploitation and forced slave labor. Going in we knew it would be a heart-wrenching trip, but we also knew God wanted us there to love and minister to the women who had been rescued out of human trafficking.

As we looked into the faces of the rescued young women, we saw their precious innocence had been shattered. We heard their stories of how family members sent them to work so they could send money back home, but instead they found themselves without their passports and literally thrown into a brothel where they were expected to "service" many men each day. They wanted freedom so badly they risked their lives to escape. The courage these girls displayed was staggering. Thankfully, they were now in a safe place, going to school or learning a trade, and hearing about the God who wants to take care of them *and* heal their hearts.

As we heard the girls each sharing their stories, we were surprised to hear so many different accents. It didn't occur to us before meeting them that they had been taken from different countries. This once again proved to us **Satan's hatred for women is global as is his intent to destroy them.** Trafficking young women for sex not only assaults them, but the God who made them.

I don't tell this to scare women or make them feel victimized or weak, quite the contrary. Women must realize *their value* makes them a lure for the enemy. Satan has been observing humans since the beginning of mankind, and he knows the damage they can do to his kingdom when they yield to God's authority and take their position. He is very real and is constantly on the prowl.

It's wise for women and men alike to keep in mind Satan is always looking for unsaved, unknowing, ignorant, or rebellious people to take up one of his evil assignments. He has a bull's-eye on females who are exposed, unprotected, desperate, or have strayed away from the safety of healthy community. But it's also wise for us to remember if God allows an attack, He has plans to use it for our good and possibly the good of others. **If God allows a battle or struggle, He promises to grow us, mature us, and show His glory in it.** The Lord promises not to waste any of our pain and to never leave us or forsake us (no matter what we think at the time). With God, nothing is over until He says it's over!

TAKING OUR POSITIONS

Knowing how vulnerable women are to the enemy makes it even more imperative for men to take their positions and stay close to the Lord. If not, they're more susceptible to an attack of the enemy, also known as spiritual warfare. Don and I have experienced this firsthand.

Soon after I was saved, the enemy picked up the pace and honed in on our family. Don had no idea Satan was real, and before he knew it, he had unknowingly taken up an assignment of the enemy, which almost destroyed our marriage. Don, who had always been pretty quiet and non-confrontational, became confused, threatened, and in time, verbally and emotionally abusive. Sometimes just the look of disgust was enough to make me want to sob! As I mentioned earlier in the book, my father had convinced him my faith had made me radical and emotionally unhealthy. He did everything he could to convince Don to leave me and take the kids. Thankfully, the Lord proved everything I had been reading in the Bible and learning in Bible study was true. Jesus held my feet on level ground and covered me, while He began to reveal Himself to Don. It would be years before Don fully knew what had happened. Once the storm blew over and the battle ceased, it scared Don to realize what he had been involved in without even knowing it. This is why we need to have accountability in small groups and pray for one another. I am a firm believer, because of personal experience, that *healthy* small groups provide this kind of support, growth, and safety.

Men and women must take their positions seriously. If we are not walking with the Lord and focused on Him, we can't possibly stand up to the insidious, evil activity of Satan. **When we are born again and walking with the Lord, the enemy can't possibly stand up against us!** *That is powerful!*

AUTHENTIC HUMILITY

Men, we've talked a lot about the influence women have, but have you considered the power you've been given? You have a tremendous ability to build value into the hearts and lives of the females in your life. Yet you also have the power to defeat, distract, discourage, and deeply hurt the women in your life, maybe even more than you realize.

As we look at the beautiful balance of authority and humility in scripture, we continually see Jesus' tenderness toward women even when it was countercultural. He was and *still is* the perfect example for all of us. Even the woman caught in adultery and the Samaritan woman at the well were offered truth with love and forgiveness. He knew how to be tender toward women and wants to teach men how to authentically respond the way He would.

Authentic humility in a man is powerful and healing. **There is nothing safer to a woman than a strong man who chooses to be emotionally tender toward her.** It's a reflection of Jesus, and women are built to be content "there." Men, God is very interested in what women become while in a man's care. As you labor through these difficult situations, you have the privilege of a ringside seat to her transformation. Cooperation with Him will also build your character and your faith dramatically!

Christian women have a tendency to cover up or push down their pain until they can't keep it down anymore. (During child rearing years, women become masters at this, not by a conscious choice but because they are so busy. They have an almost uncanny ability to be a "Queen of Denial." I speak from experience.) **The enemy watches women, and if they don't acknowledge their pain, let it be revealed so they can deal with it, talk about it, or learn to speak "truth in love," he will trigger the pain and bring it up when they least expect it.** When that happens, every painful emotion she has stuffed deep down inside comes spewing out like a hot volcano. Women don't like the way they act out, but they can't always stop it. When a female feels invisible, powerless, angry, or worthless, she will eventually cry. If she has been stuffing down the pain for years (or if her heart is full of pain), she may cry loudly and for extended periods. She may even be surprised at the sounds that come out of her. Nothing she says sounds like a language anyone can understand. Men, you need to know that often she doesn't understand what's happening either.

When a woman spews emotionally, she may be saying, "Will you please help me?" She may be full of pain or feeling empty. She may feel weak and ugly. No matter what she's feeling, she needs to know the men in her life care enough to come into this icky place to help her. She needs a man who is willing to love her right where she is.

WHAT TO DO WHEN SHE'S BEEN FRACTURED OR SHATTERED

Men, when a woman verbally or emotionally erupts like a volcano, she's telling you she's weary, raw, fractured, or completely shattered. She was not built for war in the same way you were. Don't make the mistake of expecting her to feel and respond like you; she is not a man. She is *fragile* and, in this case, the crystal pitcher is fractured and broken. Depending on the depth of the pain, she may feel as though she has had emotional heart surgery and needs time to rehab. Be gentle with her fragile heart.

If you inflict pain, you must take responsibility and own what you did to her (even if you didn't mean to and don't understand what you did). What she needs and desires is your time, attention, focus, and presence. She was made for restoration and will most likely forgive you and give you another opportunity, because she desperately wants *you.*

Dads, husbands, friends, neighbors, or bosses—this truth runs across the board and is not only helpful but imperative. When you have hurt a female's feelings, even if and especially when you have no idea what you did to hurt her feelings, just stop yourself (only if you mean it), and say, "I am really sorry I hurt your feelings." It won't be the same to *just say*, "I'm sorry." You have to own it and take responsibility even if you don't understand why it hurt her, just accept that she is different than you and when she shows pain that was inflicted by you, admit you hurt her feelings and sincerely say you are sorry. It's not easy, but it is simple! To apologize doesn't mean you are wrong, it just means you know you hurt her. Feelings are not negotiable. When people are hurt, they *feel* hurt.

WHAT A WOMAN NEEDS FOR RESTORATION

When a woman is shattered or completely shuts down, it may take hours for her to "come back to life." Healing may take days, weeks, or months. (A fracture *can* cause an affair and vice versa. If an affair has occurred, it may take *a long time* with serious prayer, work, and routine professional counseling for healing to occur.) Giving her your undivided attention and focus is a gift that she needs more than anything you can buy for her. **A woman hates being separated from her man, because it makes her feel exposed, devalued, and rejected, so be patient.**

Chances are, no matter what she says (unless you have allowed it to go on way too long), she wants restoration and needs you *and* the strength you bring. She may need you to just sit with her. Give her as much time as she needs. If she allows you to touch her in a non-sexual way, do so. Touching her may help ground her and help her focus on you instead of her pain. Stay with her for as long as it takes; it proves to her she is worth your time. Be careful though, her nerves and heart are hypersensitive to you and if she feels manipulated or hurried, it may cause further damage. If that happens, she may pull away and you will have to begin the process again. Pray and ask God for the "fruit of His Spirit" (Galatians 5:22–23). Then, obey whatever and however the Lord leads. Let her know she is your number one focus and that you will stay for as long as it takes her to "come back to life."

She may cry a lot *or* she may be silent *or* she may alternate between the two, but stay. She may ramble and say irrational things; just hold the handle of her crystal pitcher (her) and let her pour out whatever she needs to pour. If it has been building up for a long time, it may take a while, but by allowing her to pour, you are building trust. This is your opportunity to show tenderness and begin to put her shattered heart back together. If she brings up past offenses and says things she really doesn't mean, remember, it may be the fear and pain talking. Touch her, if she is open to it, because it helps bring her heart back to the center. Stay and focus until she lets go of you or walks away.

Guys, don't rush her. If it took months or years to dig into the muddy pit, it can take time to reach the ground level again. Allow time for new seeds to be consistently planted, take root, and grow. If you are silent for long, become emotionally disconnected, or raise your voice, you may shatter her heart again. *And there may be a limited number of times she can be restored to you.*

WARNING! Women, please recognize a man is as vulnerable as you are at this moment. This is very hard for him and takes great courage to walk into this emotional landmine. If a man feels manipulated or taken advantage of, he will pull back and not trust you. Please, ladies, don't make this an opportunity to suggest ways he needs to change. That can be discussed later when emotions aren't so raw. Don't take advantage of him and abuse his heart. A healthy man will be devastated, because he knows he's hurt you deeply. He doesn't enjoy hurting you (and may have done it unintentionally). He may be more sad, sorry, and afraid than you can imagine at this moment. Emotionally healthy men are much more afraid of losing the women they love than our culture suggests.

Thankfully, nothing about this situation shocks, offends, or confuses Father God! He is right there with her, holding her. And when a man finds himself in this situation with a woman, it's important to remember **God is there with him too—he is not alone.** The Holy Spirit knows what she needs; men just need to press in and follow wherever He leads. As scary as it seems, God will give men the strength and courage to walk into the pain with her. By representing Jesus to her in this way, God will use a man's arms, hands, presence, and words to bring safety and confidence to a woman in the middle of that pain. Remember, God designed her to ache for and to fit in your arms!

Husbands, consider what Jesus did for His bride—He died for her. Ask the Lord for direction, and ask Him what He wants to say to you about her and how she is feeling. He may give you a view of her or of yourself that you never expected. Ask Him what He wants to say to her and be His mouthpiece. There can be power and healing in His words, which are always more adequate than your own.

PAUSE, PONDER, PRAY, AND OBEY

MEN:

1. Have you been in the presence of a shattered female? If so, how did you respond to her?

2. Did her emotional state and response scare you?

3. How have you responded well in the past?

4. How have you responded poorly?

5. Will you respond in a different way now that you know these keys?

6. Will you be vulnerable and admit you hurt her feelings?

7. Can you walk into the pain of the moment and be like Jesus to her? If not, why not?

8. How will you prepare yourself if you see there is an opportunity to restore her?

9. Do you believe you have the power to rebuild her?

10. Do you believe you have the power to break her?

11. Do you believe you have the power to restore her?

WOMEN:

1. Can you remember a time you were completely shattered? What was the situation, and how did you feel?

2. Did your reaction surprise you?

3. When was the last time you were shocked at the sounds that were coming out of your body?

4. Was any of it because a man was not covering you or protecting you? Explain.

5. Have you ever witnessed another woman shattered?

    a. What did it feel like?

      b. Did it scare you?

      c. What did you do?

      d. Are you proud of how you responded or ashamed of how you reacted?

6. Will you respond in a different way now that you know these keys?

7. Will you be vulnerable and tell the men in your life when they hurt your feelings so it doesn't have to get to a place of erupting? Is there someone you can ask to hold you accountable? If so, when will you ask them?

8. Are you willing to allow a man you trust to walk into the pain with you and comfort you?

9. Do you believe men have the power to rebuild and restore you? If so, why? If not, why not?

What is the Holy Spirit saying to you? Take some time to find three scripture verses that encourage you or confirm what you are hearing.

_____

_____

_____

_____

_____

_____

_____

_____

_____

_____

_____

_____

_____

_____

_____

_____

_____

_____

_____

_____

_____

_____

Come to me, all you who are weary and
burdened, and I will give you rest.
Matthew 11:28 (NIV)

Chapter 8

THE WARNING: TRAPS, TRIGGERS, AND BAIT

Don has become my biggest supporter and cheerleader. I love him more today than ever before and more than I ever thought possible. He is my hero and the one the Lord used to encourage me to share this with you. He believes in the power and effectiveness of these keys of truth so much that he has partnered with me in this ministry, sowing into it financially and emotionally. Even though he is busy running two successful companies, it's very important to him for us to share what we have learned and experienced. We both want to help others avoid the pain we experienced for so many years, and it's our desire to offer you these keys of truth to unlock doors that may have been holding you captive. These truths and revelations have radically changed us individually and as a couple. Our marriage, family, and relationships with friends are stronger than ever because of these keys.

Yet, none of us are ever beyond being trapped and falling into old patterns. **God allows us to experience pain and walk through tests to give us opportunities to learn and be transformed into His image.** These situations can bring the impurities of our hearts to the surface. What I am about to share made it apparent that Don and I are, and will always be, in the process of *becoming* more like Christ. Let me explain what happened so you can be on guard and be prepared to identify traps and triggers, but have the courage to accept being used as bait.

FALLING INTO OLD PATTERNS

When I finally decided to obey the Lord and write this book, we looked at our calendars and planned time for me to take a couple of trips alone to our lake house so I could write without interruption.

About three weeks before I was scheduled to leave, Don seemed distracted and not as connected emotionally, which triggered fear in me. He was focused on and preoccupied by work. He was home physically, but not emotionally. I sensed he was falling back into an old pattern—"The Provider Trap." This felt so familiar to Don he didn't even realize he'd fallen.

Men are wired to provide, but we need to be aware that the enemy often, if not always, takes the very thing God wired into us for *Him* and uses it against us. When our giftings are not sifted through the Holy Spirit, they bring our destruction.

As the distance between us continued to grow, Don began exhibiting some old attitudes and behaviors I hadn't seen in a while. I knew if I wasn't careful, it could trigger some old behaviors in me as well. I did not want us to get caught in that familiar downward spiral.

I felt fear increasing daily as I figuratively watched Don leave the safety of our ship and climb down the ladder to his small life raft. It would be easy for me to ignore it and just let him "drift" while protecting my heart. I had practiced that for years, but I knew it was *not* productive. Quite honestly, I was horrified at the thought of him drifting off again after we had made so much progress. "Lord," I prayed, "I don't want to be disappointed or feel rejected again. Please help us get out of this unscathed."

In my mind, I knew the enemy was attacking us because I was obeying the Lord by writing this book. I had been filled with so much doubt about my ability to write; the idea alone scared me half to death. Anytime we are about to launch out in obedience and do something the Lord is asking us to do, the enemy studies our behavior and sets traps that have worked against us in the past. He's not very creative, but he'll do anything to distract us and cause us to doubt. I believed it then, and I believe it now. The enemy could see and hear I was preparing to share with the world something the Lord had downloaded into my heart. He knew it was something that could potentially save marriages, restore relationships, and heal families. He would do anything to keep these keys of truth from being brought to life.

Trap: Any device or plan for tricking a person or thing into being caught unaware; anything resembling a trick or prison.

Trigger: Any event that sets a course of action in motion.

Bait: An enticement; temptation.

THE TRAP

After months of walking in freedom, Don once again began to isolate himself emotionally by talking less and being preoccupied with business. He had gone into what I call "his emotional cave." I felt sad seeing him like this; fear and pain bubbled just below the surface of my heart. I prayed and asked the Lord to show me what was going on and what I should do. I tried a few times to wave him down as he blew by me on the fast track, seemingly in another world. But again, I made excuses for Don and conceded he had a lot going on at work. I told myself his emotional distance had nothing to do with me and I should be thankful he was focused on providing for me, but my heart really hurt and I became fearful, which triggered me to respond the way I used to.

THE TRIGGER

Don's behavior triggered me to become silent and self-protect. I have to admit if I had taken the time to sit down and gently and respectfully ask him what was going on, things could have stopped there. After a few weeks of not being able to get his attention, and just two days before I was leaving for the lake, I snapped. I mean I *really* snapped. I snapped by verbally emasculating Don in front of our adult kids. It was not nearly as brutal as it used to be and the kids did not recognize it, but Don did and so did I. I could tell by the look on his face. It was passive but still aggressive. I pulled out my sword and verbally swiped at Don, which really hurt him. All because I had allowed fear to creep back into my heart. Realizing what I'd done, I knew I needed to apologize and ask for his forgiveness. I did and he forgave me, and he asked me for forgiveness, and I forgave him.

Don said what made *him* so sad was the shock we had gone "there" again. In the years before, we had been adversaries all the time, so *he* rarely felt the acute pain I had always felt. Now, because we are partners who really care for and try to understand one another, when we fell, we fell hard *and* fast! Only this time we fell with greater speed and lost a lot more altitude. We had further to fall than we used to, and it really hurt *both* of our hearts deeply when we realized it. We shed tears that night, because we were both so sad and disappointed. We'd grown so much and really put into practice all we'd learned. When it was all over, the result was effective and rewarding for us *both*.

We began to realize in the aftermath, we had allowed ourselves to be set up. Not only had Don fallen into a trap, but I had too. I had allowed myself to be triggered when Don fell, and then I walked right into a trap set for me too.

WAS I THE BAIT?

Sometimes in our journey with the opposite gender, most especially with those we love, the Lord will allow "us" to be used as bait in their trap. Here is what I mean: **When one of us is not positioned where we should be emotionally and spiritually (for ourselves or for the other), God may allow one to be bait for the other to signal that we are off course.** It used to hurt my feelings when God would allow Don to hurt me again. I could not understand why *He would let it happen*. Sometimes the pain was almost more than I could bear, and I really wanted to leave. But as God taught us through keys of truth, I began to realize it was Don's love for me and my love for him that allowed Him to use these painful situations to get the other's attention.

For many years, as I was walking with the Lord and when Don wasn't, I would go to the Father to "tell on Don." (I thought, *Better to tattle on Don to God than everyone else in town!*) I routinely complained to God, telling Him Don was emotionally unavailable and, at times, emotionally neglectful. Sometimes in the heat of my family situation, Don would be verbally and emotionally abusive toward me out of extreme frustration. Moving in and out of these situations over and over again, I began to realize God may have allowed it to repeat itself because it was growing my faith in Jesus. Later I realized it had, in a strange way, confirmed Don's love for me because he held on, and on, and on. It seemed Don needed to recognize the pain he caused by seeing it on my face. Because of the way we're connected, God would give us a glimpse of how we hurt Him when we hurt each other. When we try to hide our pain, it only brings more pain. God calls us to be honest with one another and "speak the truth in love" (Ephesians 4:15). At times, I have been the bait for Don and other times, Don has been the bait for me.

During this most recent "baiting season," God began to reveal this truth to me on a deeper level. I sensed the Lord whisper to my heart, "Cristie, I know it hurts and disappoints you deeply and you don't understand why I continue to allow it to happen over and over. It's never been my intention for you to be abused or neglected, but know *it's Don's love for you* that allows me to use you to train him. He doesn't want to hurt you! You are the most important person in his life (whether you believe that right now or not). I can use the pain on your face to show him the pain I feel when he drifts. I weigh everything before I let it come to you and when it comes, remember I already know what you will do with it and how it will affect you. *You are stronger than you think. Choose not to fear. Be brave!* I've got you, *and* I've got this!"

When we feel hurt and taken advantage of by someone we love, it's important to remember the Lord is trusting us and inviting us to partner with Him, and He will give us the power to stand with Him until the pain subsides or until He releases us from the situation. Stretching us makes us stronger. Our part is to lean in, take our positions, and trust God with our hearts *and* the hearts of those we love. We must also listen to His instruction. God is aware and trustworthy, and He knows exactly what He is doing.

WARNING! Beware of the Lust Trap! An emotional crisis can also be a trap of the enemy for people who are unhappy in their relationships or whose marriage is weak at the time. Too often through social media, emails, work environments, business lunches, and trips, conversations can begin. Something that starts innocently, as "friends counseling friends" (about the flaws in their marriages or relationships), can slip and before they know it, it's evolved into a full-blown affair. **Beware! Wounded people can unknowingly wound people.** Men and women who are married should be very aware of the danger in counseling or being counseled by someone of the opposite gender (unless their spouse is present or with professional counseling parameters in place). Women and men who are in a pit of pain are looking for someone to care for and rescue them, and this is a very dangerous place to be. *We can become deceived and not know we are deceived.* Satan is out to kill, steal, and destroy! He plans to take the very thing wired *into us by God* and *for God* (compassion, care, and concern) and use it to try to destroy us and everything we hold sacred. Men are wired to provide and protect, so they will easily fall into a trap rescuing, providing for, and protecting a struggling female. Women are wired to be provided for and protected, so when a woman is unhappy, neglected, ignored, abandoned, or abused, she will look for a man (or woman) to provide for and protect her. Sometimes we don't know we are in danger until it's too late. Be on guard and don't fall into the trap!

REVEALING OUR PAIN

After we talked it out, shed some tears, and shared what happened with some friends who prayed over us, Don and I were quickly back on track. We were hurt but ready and determined to be more cautious and aware. He gave me permission to signal him at the first sign of him slipping, and I did the same.

Don encouraged me, even more strongly now, to go to the lake house to begin writing this book. I agreed to go and get started. Once I was safely there, unloaded, and settled in for the night with my sweet dog, Maggie, Don called to check on us. We had a very sweet and vulnerable conversation during which he said, "I believe the Lord allowed us to fall into that 'trap' so you could write about it. You have to warn people there will be traps and they will fall, but they just need to press into the Lord and one another to get to the other side. Tell people not to quit; the benefits are worth it!" His words motivated me and made me feel equipped and ready to accomplish the task ahead.

Don and I will fall again, I am sure, and you will too. **The traps will trigger reactions we will not be proud of, but it's okay. The Lord will always be there to pick us up, dust us off, dry our tears, and set us back on our feet.** We have more habits to break and a lot to learn before we find ourselves attending that last wedding feast where Jesus, the Bridegroom of heaven, will be our host. In the meantime, He will continue to be our constant companion by leading as we follow and helping us while He waits patiently for "that" day, the day He gets to come get His Bride and bring her to heaven. He is even more anxious for us to get there than we are.

PAUSE, PONDER, PRAY, AND OBEY

MEN AND WOMEN:

1. What are your triggers?

2. What are your spouse's triggers?

3. Describe a time you were triggered but handled it well?

4. Describe a time you were triggered and did not handle it well?

5. Describe a situation where you were bait for someone?

6. Describe a time someone was used as bait for you?

7. What do you usually do when you or your spouse step into a trap?

8. What do you usually do when you step into a trap, and you recognize it?

9. Now that you know the keys of truth, will you respond differently? How?

10. What are you doing to protect yourself from falling prey to the lies of the enemy?

11. Pray now and ask the Holy Spirit to bring sensitivity to traps and for the courage to be bait for someone you love, not taking it personally. Write down your prayer below.

_____

_____

_____

_____

_____

_____

What is the Holy Spirit saying to you? Take some time to find three scripture verses that encourage you or confirm what you are hearing.

_____

_____

_____

_____

_____

_____

_____

_____

_____

_____

_____

_____

_____

_____

_____

_____

_____

_____

_____

_____

_____

_____

Finally, be strong in the Lord and in the strength of his might. Put on the whole armor of God, that you may be able to stand against the schemes of the devil. For we do not wrestle against flesh and blood, but against the rulers, against the authorities, against the cosmic powers over this present darkness, against the spiritual forces of evil in the heavenly places.
Ephesians 6:10–12 (NASB)

So, if you think you are standing firm, be careful that you don't fall! No temptation has overtaken you except what is common to mankind. And God is faithful; he will not let you be tempted beyond what you can bear. But when you are tempted, he will also provide a way out so that you can endure it.
1 Corinthians 10:12–13 (NIV)

Chapter 9

POSITIONING OUR HEARTS AND MINDS FOR CHANGE

Not too long ago, I was speaking to a group about the keys of truth. When the class was over, a few people came up afterward to share their personal stories with me. Interestingly, most of the people who came forward were women who had been hurt, abused, and/or abandoned by men. One of the women who shared with me said, "My husband left me with five children. He was emotionally incapable of being a provider and protector. If I had known about these keys when we were dating, I would have known how to take my position and it would have allowed me to see he was not healthy enough to take his. I really wish I had known all of this back then." (I hear stories like this a lot. People often say, "young people need to know this *before* they get married." I wholeheartedly agree!)

What this sweet woman said taught me something of great value. As we position ourselves in the appropriate place, it is wise to watch what the opposite gender does. Old habits are hard to break, and it's only through submission to God's power that we can truly break them. **Your new position may cause some confusion and difficulty in existing relationships; it might even *end* unhealthy ones.** Repositioning takes time, and there are some men and women who are so wounded, they need professional help and ministry in order to be healed. (I am very thankful to be part of a church that believes in freedom ministry and offers freedom training to so many leaders and churches globally. I highly recommend you read more about it at freedom.gatewaypeople.com.)

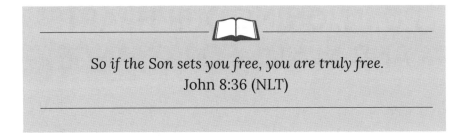

So if the Son sets you free, you are truly free.
John 8:36 (NLT)

If a relationship is new and the other person is trying to force you into a position that is not in agreement or alignment with God's plan, stop it before it gets too far. **If you sense the Holy Spirit, friends, or parents telling you it will not work or isn't healthy for some reason, have the courage to listen and respond accordingly.** When we ignore "red flags" alerting us that danger is on the horizon, we can become exhausted, entangled, and severely damaged in the end. Be brave enough to pause, ponder, pray, and obey what God is speaking to you. God designed creation with an order, and taking our positions in His order will allow us to *thrive*.

If a man or woman has personal wounds and is yielded to a spirit of rebellion, he or she probably won't be interested in the things of God or in becoming emotionally healthy or spiritually whole. If this is the case, the process will be very difficult and, more than likely, leave destruction in its wake. Ask God to give you discernment, wisdom, and the courage to see the truth about what He is putting before you. God can heal anyone who is willing to be vulnerable and teachable, but when you're not, He will not force you. He wants you to *choose Him, because He already chose you.*

Now the Lord is the Spirit, and where the Spirit of the Lord is, there is freedom. And we all, who with unveiled faces contemplate the Lord's glory, are being transformed into His image with ever-increasing glory, which comes from the Lord, who is the Spirit.
2 Corinthians 3:17–18 (NIV)

REPOSITIONING TAKES TIME

As you ponder the keys of truth and all you've learned, don't allow yourself to get bogged down reflecting on what you may have done wrong in the past. Because of our culture and the times we live in, most of us didn't know or understand God's way or it wasn't modeled for us. Remember, we are all products of our environments, and most of our environments were not perfect.

If you begin to feel convicted by the Holy Spirit, simply go to God and ask Him for forgiveness for your attitudes toward one or both genders. Ask Him to help you forgive those who did not teach you because they may not have known God's way. And ask Him to help you forgive yourself and give you peace and courage to move in cadence with Him. Then begin putting the keys into practice.

Here are a few things to keep in mind as you spend time processing and understanding the keys of truth:

1. We have been **influenced by our environments** (culture and families of origin).

2. Most of us did not know to do things any differently than what we **learned from our upbringings.**

3. Thank God for His Holy Spirit who speaks and trains us His way. Thank Him for what you now know and for new beginnings and the opportunity to grow. Thank Him for His desire and ability to transform you into His likeness as you yield to the sanctification process. **Thank Him that he doesn't focus on making us happy but holy!**

4. Remember that **change can hurt and confuse people who are close to us.** As we begin to reposition, some of the people in your life may not know how to respond to or appreciate the "new you." It may take time for them to get on board, so have patience Don't forget, the Lord may be using you to bring about change in others.

5. Things that once felt **normal and familiar may no longer feel good.**

6. **Press on and keep the big picture and God's plan in mind.** Hang on to His hand, focus on His face, and *keep doing your part* to obey by doing "the next right thing" He tells you to do. He always keeps his promises, and His timing is always perfect.

7. **Be patient** as you begin practicing these new keys. You will stumble and fall and that's okay. *Give yourself* and *others grace* as you move forward.

8. **Remember that it only takes one person to begin the repositioning** of a couple, family, workplace, organization, or culture. As we partner with God and are led by His Spirit, He will help us all the way through. We don't have to get

stuck. **Resist the urge to lean away from uncomfortable situations to protect yourself.**

9. When we don't step up and into the position God has for us, the divine design of men and women is aborted. When we ignore God's plan, individuals, families, organizations, and cultures perish. **Be bold and brave— you are not alone, you are partnering with the Creator of the Universe.**

10. Muster the courage to **get up when you fall**, even when someone you care about seems to have tripped you. **Get up. Don't give up.**

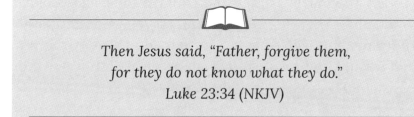

Then Jesus said, "Father, forgive them,
for they do not know what they do."
Luke 23:34 (NKJV)

A NEW TOMORROW

When we consider everything God wired men to desire and need from a woman, it's exactly what Jesus desires and needs from His bride (the Church). He longs for her to need His provision and protection and to want Him, trust Him, and honor Him by desiring His presence. **God wired women to need what He knew the bride of Christ would need.** She needs to reflect beauty and be transparent, cherished, and nurtured; collect and connect people; and pour living water over the globe, bringing forth life. Isn't our God something? He really does desire for us to be a reflection on earth as it *is* right now in Heaven.

I pray the eyes of your heart will be opened to God's relentless love and desire for you. May you see clearly the position He created for you. May we all continue to choose to reposition ourselves and value and appreciate the amazing males and females He has so graciously placed in our lives as gifts to partner with and help us be all we were created to be.

Take courage my friend. Repositioning takes commitment, requires purposefulness, and is a process. Just as it takes a while to build physical and emotional muscle memory to change habits, spiritual muscle memory is no different. However, we have the amazing help and power of the Holy Spirit of God to help us. There are many things in life we can't change on our own. This is why we have to lean into the Lord and not let fear make us turn away. Ask Him to give you ears to hear what He has to say to your heart and the courage to "pause, ponder, pray, and obey what He says." Remember, you won't get it right all the time; you will stumble and fall, but Jesus is there to extend a hand and help you get up and walk again. Will you take His hand?

CONCLUSION

You did it! You made it to the end. I hope your journey has been worthwhile and that your key ring has some shiny new keys of truth hanging from it. I pray you will use them often and they become part of your everyday life. May they help you lock the enemy out and lock you and your relationships safely in the confines of truth.

As I sit here today, I am still in awe of the amazing process of birthing these keys of truth. While I may still be learning to be brave and go when God says, "Go," He has proven His faithfulness to me through this process again and again. I know He will continue to do the same for you. **I hope He never ceases to shock us with His voice and His grace.**

As we journey through life, may He continue to increase our desire to please Him, know Him better, and love Him more.

I am so grateful that at times He overrides our humanity and gives us the "want" to obey. I am also blown away by His desire and ability to continually and consistently offer us "do-overs" (Lamentations 3:22–23).

I love how God sometimes gives us just enough information to help us say "yes." Then when we agree and decide to do as He says, we think we are saying yes because we know the entirety of the assignment. But so often, as we get a little further down the road, we realize the stakes are higher than we first thought. As we round each bend and venture a little further from what we think home base is, we begin to slow down because we think this road may require more vulnerability than we first thought. But God is good and always *gives* way more than He requires!

Our remarkable God had more than a few surprises for me during this process. As I began to walk through the keys of truth, my life unfolded before me. **As each key unlocked another door of my past, it became more and more obvious that Jesus had been standing with me all along. He was smack dab in the middle of every season and every situation, good and bad.** Through the scary process of typing out this story, Jesus sat with me and reminded me of all the ground "we" had covered together and how extraordinarily faithful He has been.

The same is true for you! He has been hovering over you all your life. He woos and pursues us, inviting us to open our hearts to him and receive His unconditional love. Somehow we know we don't deserve it, but He won't stop trying to convince us. Once we stop running, He comes promising to never leave us or forsake us.

So, thank you! Thank you for the opportunity to take this journey and for the opportunity to share these keys of truth with you. Thank you for allowing me to stir in portions of my life and God's goodness to our family. **I believe God uses our history and pain to help others.** My intent was to help people by sharing what has helped me, but in God's multifaceted way, He was doing more than one or two things at one time. His timing is always perfect, even when it doesn't seem that way. When we keep our eyes and hearts focused on Him, He is happy to show us His glory.

I am so thankful God offers all of us the strength to hang on and work through situations and seasons in our families that we sometimes believe will kill us. I am also thankful God helps us not to bail from being one another's "bait," because *the results are worth it.*

I pray what God has revealed here will be a valuable tool to you. May it pour courage into you, equip you, and empower you to live your life in line with the original design put in place by God the Father who loves us more than we imagine. May we all keep the big picture in mind until we see Him face-to-face in the throne room of Heaven!

But if we hope for what we do not yet have, we wait for it patiently. In the same way, the Spirit helps us in our weakness. We do not know what we ought to pray for, but the Spirit himself intercedes for us through wordless groans. And he who searches our hearts knows the mind of the Spirit, because the Spirit intercedes for God's people in accordance with the will of God. **And we know that in all things God works for the good of those who love him, who have been called according to his purpose.**
Romans 8:25–28 (NIV, emphasis added)

PAUSE, PONDER, PRAY, AND OBEY

MEN AND WOMEN:

1. Are you willing to reposition? Are you willing to admit there were some things that you did not know?

2. Will you choose to be courageous enough to move into a place that may be new and challenging to you?

3. Will you pray and ask the Lord to reveal any pride or fear you might have in your heart that could threaten to immobilize you?

4. Will you let go of the past hurts and move forward trusting the Lord to help you do your part?

5. Will you start believing that men and women are made by God to partner with one another?

6. Will you lay down your swords and believe the best about each other?

7. Will you stop accepting the world's stance about males and females and instead focus on what God's Word says?

What is the Holy Spirit saying to you? Take some time to find three scripture verses that encourage you or confirm what you are hearing.

_____

_____

_____

_____

_____

_____

_____

_____

_____

_____

_____

_____

_____

_____

_____

_____

_____

_____

_____

I pray that out of his glorious riches he may strengthen
you with power through his Spirit in your inner being,
so that Christ may dwell in your hearts through faith.
And I pray that you, being rooted and established in love,
may have power, together with all the Lord's holy people,
to grasp how wide and long and high and deep is the
love of Christ, and to know this love that surpasses
knowledge—that you may be filled to the measure
of all the fullness of God. **Now to him who is able to
do immeasurably more than all we ask or imagine,
according to his power that is at work within us, to
him be glory in the church and in Christ Jesus
throughout all generations, for ever and ever! Amen.**
Ephesians 3:16–21 (NIV, emphasis added)

Do nothing out of selfish ambition or vain conceit.
Rather, in humility value others above yourselves, not
looking to your own interests but each of you to the
interests of the others. In your relationships with one
another, have the same mindset as Christ Jesus.
Philippians 2:3–5 (NIV)

But the fruit of the Spirit is love, joy, peace, forbearance,
kindness, goodness, faithfulness, gentleness and
self-control. Against such things there is no law. Those
who belong to Christ Jesus have crucified the flesh with
its passions and desires. Since we live by the Spirit, let
us keep in step with the Spirit. Let us not become
conceited, provoking and envying each other.
Galatians 5:22–26 (NIV)

AFTERWORD: ONE LAST THING

A few months ago, Don and I had the pleasure of taking another cruise, this time with our family. It was our first family vacation with *all* of our adult children. A few months earlier, when Don and I went on our first cruise alone, we met Eileen, Senior Executive Administrator to the President & CEO of Royal Caribbean International. We became fast friends and kept in touch after we got home. Because of her, all six of us received *royal* treatment on this cruise. I don't say this to brag, but to remind us all our Heavenly Father is *always* looking for ways to bless His kids, get our attention, and reveal Himself to us in a personal way. He used our new friend Eileen to do just that. Like me, you've probably noticed God is multifaceted and rarely does just *one thing* at a time. He is always moving!

All six of us packed our bags, flew from Dallas/Fort Worth to Florida, and boarded the Celebrity Silhouette, a 122,210-ton, 2,886-passenger liner with 1,500 crew members. We were all excited, but especially excited for our son-in-law, Jon, who had never cruised before. We settled into our staterooms and then walked around exploring the ship.

As the week progressed, we realized we were getting a level of service we could never buy. (Sometimes it was a little hard to receive, honestly. Who were we to be treated with such exceptional care and honor? We knew we had done nothing to deserve it.) Evidently, our new friend had arranged many surprises for us, but one was to be guests at the captain's table for dinner.

On the first formal night, we were greeted by the captain and escorted down a *two-story* grand staircase to his table in the center of the room. All of us were thinking the same thing: *Who are we to get this kind of treatment?* We were then seated at the table where each of us had a place card with our name printed on it. Our chairs were pulled out for us, and our napkins were placed in our laps. My seat was on the left side of the distinguished Greek captain, which allowed for Don and I to have one-on-one conversations with him. It was a delightful evening! During dinner, the captain extended a personal invitation for us all to join him for a private tour of the bridge, which is where the officers pilot the ship. During our dinner conversation, Don asked some questions about the ship and the Captain discovered Don was an engineer, so he arranged for the guys to have a private tour of the engine control room. They were *blown away* at the sophistication of the ship's systems.

So, what is my point in sharing all of this with you? It's to show that once you catch on to the keys of truth, you begin seeing them in every area of your life.

Whether we were dining around the captain's table or standing at the helm on the bridge, I sensed a stirring in my heart and soul. Every officer on the bridge, with one exception, was a male, and every time they spoke about the ship, they referred to it as a "she." Phrases like, "She is a remarkable." "She is powerful." "She is beautiful, elegant, sophisticated, amazing ...." You get the idea.

During this cruise, we had the first draft of this book to read through and edit, cover to cover. Maybe it's because it was fresh on my mind, but the night after the captain's dinner, I woke up and sensed the Lord stirring me, wanting to speak to me. I felt He was trying to show me something symbolically. This experience further solidified the principles and truths found in this book.

THE SILHOUETTE

Women are very much like the Silhouette. They are amazingly designed, beautifully fashioned, and full of grace. They are able to provide calm, comfort, transport, and safety.

Like the beautiful Silhouette, they are strong and sturdy having the ability to stay together in wind and waves and power through rough seas. They can gently rock people to sleep and bring comfort and rest. They can dock at different ports all over the globe when handled with care, wisdom, and respect and, yes, training and experience. Like the Silhouette, women can deteriorate, rust, cease to run, or crash into a pier (or other foreign objects) if not cared for and handled with great respect for both her power and fragility.

THE CAPTAIN

As we stood on the bridge, we saw the seriousness of the captain and the great responsibility he felt for his ship. We saw the pride and care he takes when she is under his watch. The bridge was spotless and every instrument was perfectly equilibrated, calibrated, and balanced. These men are constantly monitoring her radar and gages for currents, depths, threatening weather, or foreign vessels in the vicinity. The captain or one of his crew is awake, focused, and on duty *at all times*. Their job and focus is on caring for, maintaining, and protecting *her*, and they all take it seriously.

Order and submission to authority is important to the safety of every ship on the water and to every passenger onboard. We could all rest easy during the day and go to sleep at night knowing even in the dark, the men on the bridge were at their posts and focused on doing their jobs. And if need be, our captain would sleep with one eye open to monitor the computer screens that hung on the wall beside his bed.

I'm so thankful the Lord made men and women so different *and* so necessary for each other! Just as a ship needs her captain, a woman needs a man to navigate and care for her. She functions better and feels safer when those who are responsible for her not only do their jobs well, with honor and respect, but have earned the privilege of caring for her by following the required protocol.

KEEPING AN ATTITUDE OF GRATITUDE

It's so important we don't take *anything* for granted. In fact, God asks for us to bring Him "a sacrifice of praise" (Hebrews 13:15, NIV). It's good for us to be thankful to God for how He made us and how we can work together to make each other better. Don't allow negativity to darken your thoughts and your mind. The enemy will use that to come against you. Instead, boldly and confidently approach the throne of God with thanksgiving and praise. His light and love will pour into you and transform you.

I will offer to You the sacrifice of thanksgiving,
and will call upon the name of the Lord.
Psalm 116:17 (NKJV)

For so long, I questioned how I could have been in church for 36 years and seeking God, yet missed Him. I knew about religion, but I didn't have a personal relationship with Him. Why did it take so long for me to receive truth that would not only change my life, but *save me.* I spent a lot of time questioning and asking God why it took so long, but what He clearly showed me is that **when there is lack, there is always an exchange of gratitude when we receive what we have been yearning for.** So regardless of where you started when you began this journey, I hope you're thankful for what you've gleaned from the keys of truth.

As you finish this book and begin letting it soak in, I believe you'll start seeing every relationship, friendship, and partnership you have in a new light. As you begin implementing the keys of truth and treating the opposite sex differently, I pray you begin to sense a strong and growing sense of gratitude and thanksgiving to God for His design and plan for you!

Now to him who is able to do immeasurably more than all we ask or imagine, according to his power that is at work within us, to him be glory in the church and in Christ Jesus throughout all generations, for ever and ever! Amen.
Ephesians 3:20–21 (NIV)

You'll remember, friends, that when I first came to you to let you in on God's master stroke, I didn't try to impress you with polished speeches and the latest philosophy. I deliberately kept it plain and simple: first Jesus and who he is; then Jesus and what he did—Jesus crucified.

I was unsure of how to go about this, and felt totally inadequate—I was scared to death, if you want the truth of it—and so nothing I said could have impressed you or anyone else. But the Message came through anyway. God's Spirit and God's power did it, which made it clear that your life of faith is a response to God's power, not to some fancy mental or emotional footwork by me or anyone else.

We, of course, have plenty of wisdom to pass on to you once you get your feet on firm spiritual ground, but it's not popular wisdom, the fashionable wisdom of high-priced experts that will be out-of-date in a year or so. God's wisdom is something mysterious that goes deep into the interior of his purposes. You don't find it lying around on the surface. It's not the latest message, but more like the oldest—what God determined as the way to bring out his best in us, long before we ever arrived on the scene. The experts of our day haven't a clue about what this eternal plan is. If they had, they wouldn't have killed the Master of the God-designed life on a cross. That's why we have this Scripture text:

No one's ever seen or heard anything like this,

Never so much as imagined anything quite like it—

What God has arranged for those who love him.

But you've seen and heard it because God by his Spirit has brought it all out into the open before you.

The Spirit, not content to flit around on the surface, dives into the depths of God, and brings out what God planned all along. Who ever knows what you're thinking and planning except you yourself? The same with God—except that he not only knows what he's thinking, but he lets us in on it. God offers a full report on the gifts of life and salvation that he is giving us. We don't have to rely on the world's guesses and opinions. We didn't learn this by reading books or going to school; we learned it from God, who taught us person-to-person through Jesus, and we're passing it on to you in the same firsthand, personal way.

The unspiritual self, just as it is by nature, can't receive the gifts of God's Spirit. There's no capacity for them. They seem like so much silliness. Spirit can be known only by spirit—God's Spirit and our spirits in open communion. Spiritually alive, we have access to everything God's Spirit is doing, and can't be judged by unspiritual critics. Isaiah's question, "Is there anyone around who knows God's Spirit, anyone who knows what he is doing?" has been answered: Christ knows, and we have Christ's Spirit.
1 Corinthians 2:1–16 (MSG)

What is the Holy Spirit saying to you?

_____

_____

_____

_____

_____

How have you changed since you began learning the keys of truth?

_____

_____

_____

_____

_____

Is there anything you want to say to God right now? Feel free to write out a prayer below or stop and say a prayer to the Lord. Be honest with Him. He wants you to be real and authentic. If there's an area of your life that needs clarity or strength, feel free to lay it out before Him. He loves to hear from His children!

_____

_____

_____

_____

_____

Take some time to find three scriptures that encourage you or confirm what you're hearing and write them below.

1. _____

_____

_____

_____

_____

_____

_____

2. _____

_____

_____

_____

_____

_____

_____

_____

_____

3. _____

_____

_____

_____

_____

_____

_____

_____

_____

_____

"Ah, Sovereign Lord, you have made the heavens and
the earth by your great power and outstretched
arm. Nothing is too hard for you."
Jeremiah 32:17 (NIV)

But if we walk in the light, as he is in the light, we
have fellowship with one another, and the blood
of Jesus, His Son, purifies us from all sin.
1 John 1:7 (NIV)

SUGGESTED RESOURCES

James C. Dobson

Bringing Up Boys. Tyndale Momentum; Reissue edition, August 22, 2014.

Bringing Up Girls. Tyndale Momentum; Reprint edition, August 22, 2014.

John Eldredge

Wild at Heart Revised and Updated: Discovering the Secret of a Man's Soul. Thomas Nelson; Rev Exp edition, April 10, 2011.

John and Stasi Eldredge

Captivating Revised and Updated: Unveiling the Mystery of a Woman's Soul. Thomas Nelson; Rev Exp edition, April 10, 2011.

Dr. Tony Evans

The Kingdom Family 6-message CD series. The Urban Alternative, 2015. tonyevans.org

Craig Groeschel

Fight: Winning the Battles That Matter Most. Zondervan, October 22, 2013.

Meg Meeker, MD

Strong Fathers, Strong Daughters: 10 Secrets Every Father Should Know. Ballantine Books; Reprint edition, August 28, 2007.

The 10 Habits of Happy Mothers: Reclaiming Our Passion, Purpose, and Sanity. Ballantine Books; 1 edition, September 6, 2011.

Robert Morris

Truly Free: Breaking the Snares That So Easily Entangle. Nashville, TN: W Publishing Group, an imprint of Thomas Nelson, 2015.

The Power of Your Words: God Will Bless Your Life Through the Words You Speak. Bloomington, MN: Bethany House, 2009, 2014.

Sarah Sumner, PhD

Men and Women in the Church. Madison WI: InterVarsity Press, 2003.

TESTIMONIALS

"*Keys of Truth* exposes the lies that both men and women believe and provides principles that are simple, yet so profound. We decided to embrace these principles, which has been the catalyst for breakthrough in our marriage. Both of us have a greater understanding of how important it is for us to function in our God-given roles to have a healthy, joyful, and fruitful marriage. Our home has been transformed, our marriage renewed, and our children are seeing what a godly marriage should look like."

Lee and Christy

"In a culture of redefining marriage and relationships, we find ourselves grabbing almost anything to give us clarity for coping with this new normal. The rise in divorce, abuse, dysfunction, capitulation, and acceptance is foundational to the unraveling of the marriage relationship that God created us for. *Keys of Truth* is an anointed teaching that provides a focus on the truths of His purpose in our design as men and women. I walked away with a refreshing understanding that my wife is wonderfully made and absolutely normal. I have a greater awareness of her fears and needs. I highly recommend *Keys of Truth* as a brilliant new teaching, not just another marriage/relationship book."

Sonny Gann (Author and Counselor)

"I am so thankful to God for Cristie's powerful and timely teaching about His design for women and men. Her explanation and encouragement helped me 'put down my sword' and understand how to be *constructive* in my marriage after years of being *destructive* out of fear. Furthermore, hearing how men need transition time and distance themselves from women who criticize revolutionized my marriage and removed so much tension. Cristie's insight is a gift to the body of Christ that everyone needs to know!"

Alexandra

"This is a resounding endorsement for *Keys of Truth* as seen through the eyes of an older man.

Men: *Keys of Truth* will immediately display a treasure trove of wisdom that carries the reader on a continuous "aha experience." The truths found in this book will not wane with time but will grow in value as the reader reflects on this resource as a life tool. You will be riveted to this book as it focuses on that which distinguishes us as men. Its thrust will not require explanation. You will intuitively know these are the missing keys stripped from us by current-day society.

Men & Women: The keys in this book will change your world. The opportunity for you to discover the keys of truth is before you. Seize the keys, and seize the moment.

Readers will find the presentation of these keys beg the question, why was the timing of this amazing gift constrained to the present season. I submit that God is never early; God is never late; God is *always* on time. The season for *Keys of Truth* is upon us.

The keys in this book will forever change your world ... and those who follow after you."

Harold

"*Keys of Truth* has helped tear down walls in our marriage we didn't even know existed! The biblical truths taught in *Keys of Truth* not only helped us to relate to one another better but also changed the way we relate to our kids. God designed us so differently, but when we function in the way we are designed, it's amazing how strongly we can function in unity!"

Traci

"We have been blessed with a terrific marriage for 30 years, so why would I need to read *Keys of Truth* or attend a Keys of Truth Conference, especially since I had this marriage and relationship thing all figured out? Well, let me tell you why: *Keys of Truth* is profoundly eye-opening and relationship changing. Cristie presented the information in a relatable and effective manner that enabled me to immediately develop a deeper appreciation and understanding of how God wired women and men. In fact, the keys are simple and practical, yet profound at the same time. When Cristie described how God wired females, I was able to see my wife in a new and clearer light. Bottom line: *Keys of Truth* is a must read and her conference is a must attend for all men who desire to enhance their understanding of and deepen their relationship with their wives and daughters."

Mark

"Cristie Penn is sharing a *fresh word* from God. Her words inspired me as a woman, a mother, and a daughter. I truly believe it will inspire you to a closer relationship with God and a chance to get a glimpse of how valuable you are to Him. Thank you, Cristie, for your obedience to God in sharing these keys of truth!"

Cathi

"I am not even sure I can put into words how impactful *Keys of Truth* has been to my marriage. As an example, knowing the physical fear my wife feels throughout the day was revelatory to me and helped me understand why she acts the way she does, especially when I am driving. This has allowed me to handle the situation in a more understanding way as opposed to taking it as a judgment on my driving.

I have been to two Keys of Truth conferences and attended Keys of Truth classes at church, and having just read the book, I can honestly say I see and hear something new every time. I think couples should commit to reading this book together at the beginning of every year to set the foundation for the New Year."

Marc

"As a single woman ... who didn't identify as 'feminine,' I have deeply struggled with feeling out of place and as if something was wrong with me. *Keys of Truth* has helped me understand myself better and has redefined femininity for me. Previous attempts to search for answers have resulted in a pattern of choosing unhealthy and controlling relationships, but *Keys of Truth* has helped enlighten me and break the patterns that have been the source of much hurt and pain in my life. Thank you, Cristie, for attentively listening to the voice of the Spirit and allowing God to use you as a vessel to share these truths."

Brandy

"My wife and I have been married for 47 years. While I love my wife and our marriage is indescribably beautiful, I was missing an important component—*understanding*. I knew she was different (and I liked that of course), but I didn't realize how God had gifted us both in ways that fully complement one another and which help us to fulfill the unique plan he has for us. In His wisdom, God fashioned us to fit together in ways that reveal Him to the world and make living life together, with someone so different, the best adventure in the world. Understanding and appreciating His unique design, gifts, roles, and calling in a marriage relationship changes everything."

John

"I thought I had to be a strong woman and in control at all times because men were weak and useless. This book changed *all* that!"

Patrice

"From the most pure and genuine place in my heart, the benefit of implementing the keys of truth has helped me discover a *love* and *trust* for my husband like I've never known or experienced before."

Fran

"My husband and I have been married for seven years. It is the second marriage for both of us. Being raised in a non-Christian family, coming to Christ in my 30s, having a father who was very distant, plus the failure of my first marriage, I had a very distorted image of men. I had no idea how to relate to my husband or son in a godly way.

I constantly asked myself, 'What does a godly man look like?' 'What does true submission to my husband look like?'

As a new believer, I felt a lot of frustration with the teachings I heard in church because none of them were giving me tools to bring real change. I tried but just didn't understand.

Keys of Truth has helped me finally find answers I had been searching for.

Learning about the female fear factor and how different fear is for females than males changed my perspective and how I see my spouse and my nine-year-old son.

Learning hero language has also changed my life as well as many other helpful and real tools that changed my distorted view and made things much more clear.

Allowing God to remove my desire to self-protect and cover myself has been revolutionary. Having experienced the disappointment of a failed marriage before I was a believer, I asked the Lord to help me have a marriage that glorifies Him. He has used *Keys of Truth* to do just that. God has used the keys to reposition my mind and heart, which allows my mate to take his position and cover and protect me. Seeing 'a hero in the making' in my nine-year-old son has given me the confidence to have a healthy relationship with him and to speak to him in a way that will call forth his masculinity and manhood as he grows. I had no way of knowing that before I had these valuable keys. This teaching has changed my perspective in a revolutionary way. Seeing my husband with new lenses has changed our marriage.

Thank you, Cristie, for this teaching! It has changed all of our lives!"

Nataliya

ACKNOWLEDGMENTS

First, I want to thank the Lord. Only He knows what it took to bring this book to life. People had suggested I write, and some even spoke it over me, but nothing inside of me desired to do it. I did not believe I was *capable* or *called to do so*. However, God can be rather persistent and quite determined to get what He wants done, *done!* I must say though, I am grateful for His persistence and for this amazing opportunity. He always knows exactly *what we need*.

This process has been hard and discouragement nipped at my heels from places I would have *never* expected it, but as God promised, the experience changed me and my relationship with Him has grown exponentially.

I marvel at the time it takes for a seed to be planted and gently cultivated by our Creator. The book you are holding in your hands was much the same process and could only have been written with God, under His direction and because of Him.

I praise God and thank Him for allowing pain in our lives to do the work it needs to do. I praise Jesus for saving me from myself and from the snares set before me even before I was born. I would be dead without Him. (We all would!)

I thank Jesus, the Great Shepherd for the protection He's provided throughout the process of writing this book. Often the warfare against it was brutal. I'm thankful He "who is in [me] is greater than he who is in the world" (1 John 4:4, NIV). Thank you, Jesus, for living inside of me and being my best friend, constant companion, and the battle commander of my life.

DON, thank you for your patience, encouragement, and constant push to share these truths that transformed our marriage and every relationship we have. Thank you for yielding to the Holy Spirit and becoming the man He made you to be, *for me and for Him*. Thank you for the unrelenting support you give to our family and for never wavering. Thank you for helping birth Keys of Truth Ministry and for constantly encouraging me to share these life-changing keys with whoever will listen. Your emotional, physical, spiritual, and financial covering made this book and ministry possible. I love you more today than I ever dreamed I could. Thank you for loving me, and others, so well.

PASTORS ROBERT AND DEBBIE MORRIS, your love for people and desire for them to be saved and live freely by the power of the Holy Spirit is contagious! Pastor Robert, it's easy to follow your strong, kind shepherd's heart. You are such an example of a man who knows how to walk the balance of *humility and authority* and lead accordingly. Thank you for making it so easy to come under your leadership because of your integrity and authenticity. Thank you for being the same man *off* the platform as you are *on*. Thank you, Pastor Debbie, for showing the women of Gateway how to live by faith, with power and humility. Your leadership style of grace and strength is rare and calls us all higher and deeper. Thank you both for listening to the *Keys of Truth* vision, supporting us, covering us, and praying for us. Thank you Pastor Robert for the words of life you've spoken over me and for the prayers you have prayed for us. Thank you for obeying the Lord and starting Gateway Church and never wavering from what God told you to do when you first began it with him. We love you both more than you know and continue to fervently pray for you.

STACY BURNETT, you have become so much more than my wordsmith, organizer, and investigator of my heart and mind—you have become my true and authentic friend! Your professionalism, patience, strength, teachable heart, and talents have been what the Lord has used as glue to hold me together through this tedious process. I still can't believe God told you to say "Yes" to us! I thank Him often for not letting you know what you were signing up for and how long it would take. I am forever grateful for the hours (and hours) we spent together pouring over years of experiences and looking for words and ways to articulate it to people of all ages and stages in a way they could understand. Thank you for fasting and praying with me every Monday for months and for being so focused on honoring our God with truth. Without you, this book would not be anything close to what it is today. I respect you more than you can imagine and value you not only as a writer and sister in Christ, but also as a priceless and precious friend. And, thank you to your amazing husband and gentle giant, Travis, for what he sacrificed for the kingdom in this project too!

PASTOR LYNDA GROVE, thank you for believing in me, even when I didn't. Thank you for giving me opportunities to learn. Thank you for the opportunities to go on mission trips overseas and for allowing me to see people need to hear what God called me to share—even in Japan! Your constant direction, grace, and encouragement have solidified the message, brought clarity, equipped me, and lifted me higher in ways I don't even understand nor can I articulate. Thank you for believing in my ability to hear God and obey. Thank you for every opportunity you have given me to soar. You make me feel covered, equipped, and more *able to obey*—even when I have to do it scared! You are an extraordinary leader, and I am honored to serve with you *and* to call you my friend.

FRAN AND MARC FISCHER, thank you for your friendship and commitment to love and support Don and me *and* Keys of Truth Ministry. Thank you for all those evenings in the very beginning when you both poured courage into me, coaching me to just take another step. Thank you for the times you lifted my face to point me back to the One we are doing this with and reminding me of those we are doing it for. Your friendship, dedication, and constant prayer coverage for us and the ministry are indescribably valuable. Thank you for never missing an opportunity to come together and pray or to come early to a conference to pray and work. I love and appreciate you both so much. Thank you for holding my feet on The Rock when I was scared and wanting to run. We are honored to do life with you.

TODD AND NATALIYA REHNQUIST, thank you for your friendship and unconditional love. When I think of how God brought us all together, I still smile, and I think Jesus does too. Thank you for the way you picked up *The Narrow Road Bible Study* as God began the slow transition in our lives from one thing to another. You created such a safe environment for so many people. Thank you both for being so teachable and for leading and following so faithfully wherever He calls you. Thank you for allowing the Lord to use you to teach so many of us through your obedience and sacrifice of time, talents, and resources. Thank you for relocating to attend Gateway Church. We can't imagine our lives without both of you.

GLORY GIRLS BIBLE STUDY, BEVERLY LEE, MARCIE MOORE, AND THE AMAZING STAFF (PAST AND PRESENT), this book would not exist without the ministry experiences of women's Bible study. May He continue to grow you and bless you all for "loving one another" so well. You will all forever be part of my heart. I love you so much.

THE NARROW ROAD BIBLE STUDY AND STAFF, I can't imagine what we *all* would have missed if the Lord had not birthed this group. The men and women who attended were, and always will be, such treasures to us. The lessons we learned by studying with you were truly life changing. God used single and married men and women (together) to raise the veil and show me some amazing truths. Some of the greatest moments in my life of ministry happened when we were all together in the upper room. Studying the Word of God *together* as men and women is, and I believe always will be, one of the greatest privileges of my life. Thank you all for sharing your lives with us. I love you and look forward to heaven with all of you.

KEYS OF TRUTH PRAYER TEAM, you know who you are. I hope you know how much I love and appreciate your commitment and dedication to the Lord. Without you, there would not be a ministry or a book. Thank you for your continued support, but most of all, thanks for the hours you have prayed and for taking it so seriously. The Lord teaches me volumes as I walk with you. Thank you for taking time out of your busy schedules to come pray before conferences and classes. Thank you for the classes you've attended and for your support and belief in the message and the ministry. Your eagerness to serve and minister in any capacity needed has been extraordinary. Thank you! Your prayers are priceless and I love you and value each one of you immeasurably, more than you can imagine.

SALLY WALTER, last, but not least, I want to thank the Lord for Sally Ann Walter. She is the precious little lady who walked into our lives to babysit our three-month-old baby boy and never left, even all these years later. *She is my hero.* She raised her son and daughter alone after her husband passed away suddenly from cancer. She was already a believer and following Jesus when I met her, and she knew I had no idea who He really was, even though I went to church every week. She invited me to an Easter pageant in 1987 where I saw the life and ministry of Christ played out on stage. She was with me when I began to weep, not stopping for hours. She was the one who invited me into the presence of God so He could introduce Himself to me. She is the one who bought both of our kids their first Bibles. She is the one who stood in for grandparents at both of our children's weddings. She is the one who loved me when I was unlovable. She is the one who cared enough to invite me to "her" church—even though I was hostile because I had heard they were "Bible thumpers." Now I am proud to be one! I praise Jesus for Aunt Sally and look forward to spending eternity with her in heaven, when the Lord calls us home.

NOTES

[1] Adapted from Gateway Church's website: http://freedom.gatewaypeople.com (accessed: July 06, 2015).

[2] *Bringing Up Girls* by James C. Dobson. Tyndale Momentum; Reprint edition, August 22, 2014.

[3] Emasculate. Dictionary.com. Dictionary.com Unabridged Random House, Inc. http://dictionary.reference.com/browse/emasculate (accessed: July 06, 2015).

[4] "Understanding the Differences Between Men and Women," Taken from the book, *If Only He Knew: What No Woman Can Resist* written by Dr. Gary Smalley and Steve Scott, published by Zondervan Publishing, http://marriagemissions.com/understanding-the-differences-between-men-and-women/ (accessed: July 20, 2015).

[5] Submission. Dictionary.com. Dictionary.com Unabridged. Random House, Inc. http://dictionary.reference.com/browse/submission (accessed: July 06, 2015).

[6] "Mental health: a state of well-being," World Health Organization. http://www.who.int/features/factfiles/mental_health/en (accessed: July 06, 2015).

[7] "Male and Female Brains Wired Differently, Scans Reveal" by Ian Sample, *The Guardian*. http://theguardian.com/science/2013/dec/02/men-women-brains-wired-differently (accessed: July 06, 2015).

[8] "Sex Differences in the Structural Connectome of the Human Brain" Edited by Charles Gross, Princeton University, Princeton, NJ, and approved November 1, 2013 (received for review September 9, 2013), Proceedings of the National Academy of Sciences of the United States of America. http://pnas.org/content/111/2/823 (accessed: July 06, 2015).

[9] "Is a Man's Skin Really Different?" by Dr. Diana Howard, *The International Dermal Institute, Inc.* (*The International Dermal Institute*). http://dermalinstitute.com/us/library/17_article_Is_a_Man_s_Skin_Really_Different_.html (accessed: July 06, 2015).

[10] "What You Should Know About Living Together," First Things First. http://firstthings.org/what-you-should-know-about-living-together (accessed: August 23, 2015).

[11] *Wild at Heart Revised and Updated: Discovering the Secret of a Man's Soul* by John Eldredge. Thomas Nelson; Rev Exp edition, April 10, 2011.

[12] "Depression in Women: Causes, Symptoms, Treatment, and Self-Help" http://www.helpguide.org/articles/depression/depression-in-women.htm (accessed: July 29, 2015).

[13] *Captivating Revised and Updated: Unveiling the Mystery of a Woman's Soul* by John and Stasi Eldredge. Thomas Nelson; Rev Exp edition, April 10, 2011.

Our son Jonathan and his wife Laura; Don and me;
Our daughter Holly and her husband Jon Piorkowski.

Taken on our family cruise, March 2015.

ABOUT THE AUTHOR

Cristie Penn is a wife, mom, creative, and teacher with a passion to communicate God's truths about how our unique gender differences are not weapons for war but rather tools for teamwork that should be celebrated. The vision for *Keys of Truth* was birthed from Cristie's 36-year marriage, the adventure of raising her son and daughter, as well as teaching and sharing biblical principles in small and large group studies throughout the past two decades. In recent years, God has sharpened her focus on the dysfunctional interactions between males and females of all ages in families, workplaces, and personal relationships. Her passion is to help these dysfunctional relationships move from frustration to partnership where the love of Christ abounds between the genders.